# Common Core
# Standards For Parents

FOR

## DUMMIES®

A Wiley Brand

## by Jared Myracle

FOR

## DUMMIES®

A Wiley Brand

**Common Core Standards For Parents For Dummies®**

Published by:
**John Wiley & Sons, Inc.,**
111 River Street,
Hoboken, NJ 07030-5774,
www.wiley.com

For general information on our other products and services, please contact our Customer Care Department within the U.S. at 877-762-2974, outside the U.S. at 317-572-3993, or fax 317-572-4002. For technical support, please visit www.wiley.com/techsupport.

Wiley publishes in a variety of print and electronic formats and by print-on-demand. Some material included with standard print versions of this book may not be included in e-books or in print-on-demand. If this book refers to media such as a CD or DVD that is not included in the version you purchased, you may download this material at http://booksupport.wiley.com. For more information about Wiley products, visit www.wiley.com.

Library of Congress Control Number: 2013954234

ISBN 978-1-118-84187-9 (pbk); ISBN 2 (ebk) 1-1180-84183-2; ISBN (ebk) 978-1-118-84174-7; ISBN (ebk) 978-1-118-84185-3

Manufactured in the United States of America

10  9  8  7  6  5  4  3  2  1

# Table of Contents

## Chapter 8: Raising the Bar: English Language Arts Standards in Grades 6–12......................147

## Chapter 9: Mastering Literacy in History/Social Studies, Science, and Technical Subjects ....... 165

## Part III: Part of Tens ................................................. 175

### Chapter 10: Ten Tips for Parents. ................... 177

# Introduction

● ● ● ● ● ● ● ● ● ● ● ● ● ● ● ● ● ● ● ● ● ● ● ● ● ● ● ● ● ● ● ● ● ● ● ● ● ● ● ● ●

**C**ongratulations. If you're reading this paragraph, you've decided to play an active role in your child's education, or you're at least taking a general interest in education. Regardless of your motivation, both actions are commendable. If this book is your first encounter with the Common Core Standards, then you're in for some useful (and understandable) information. If you're no stranger to the standards, you'll find practical applications for the standards and other tips to maximize your child's education.

Why should you be interested in academic standards? At the time of this book's writing, all but five U.S. states have adopted these standards. That's a pretty significant reason in and of itself. Probably of more interest to you, however, is the fact that your child's teachers are using these standards every day in class. To support your child's education when he comes home in the afternoons, you need to have a pretty good understanding of what he is expected to do at school.

This is where *Common Core Standards For Parents For Dummies* comes in. With tips on helping your child with schoolwork, overviews of the Common Core Standards for each grade level, and plenty of examples of how to practice the standards at home, you'll gather a wealth of resources by reading this jampacked book. So what are you waiting for?

## About This Book

This book is designed for parents, educators, and others who are interested in the Common Core Standards and their use in schools. For parents reading this book, the following pages contain many tips on creating a home environment conducive to education and offer a straightforward explanation of the standards. If you're an educator, you'll come away with many ideas on how to engage parents and help them support their children's education, particularly with regard to their mastery of the expectations within the standards.

What you won't find in this book are a bunch of unrealistic ideas that you won't be able to use at home. This book was written with a few specific goals in mind. Along with providing an understandable description of the skills and content contained in the Common Core Standards, I also try to provide recommendations that lead you to think, "Hey, we can do this." As you read different chapters, you'll find evidence of this, regardless of your child's age.

As an educator who works with students, parents, and teachers on a daily basis, I think it's important that this book leaves you feeling comfortable with understanding the Common Core Standards and beginning to work with your child to ensure his progress. However, a book can never replace a great relationship with your child's teachers and the importance of playing an active role in your child's education. That's why I provide numerous ideas for questions to ask teachers and opportunities to get involved at your child's school.

# Foolish Assumptions

In writing this book, I made some assumptions about who would be thumbing through its pages, highlighter in hand. More than likely, you'll fall into one or more of these categories:

- ✓ **You're a parent or guardian of a child in grades K–12.** I wrote this book to bring parents up to speed on the Common Core Standards and to explain your role in helping your child/student achieve those standards.

- ✓ **You know little or nothing about the Common Core Standards.** To be sure that I cover everything you need to know about Common Core, I assume that you know nothing. If you do know something about Common Core, feel free to skip the info you already know.

- ✓ **You're looking for specific ways to support your child's education at home.** I made every effort to progress quickly to ideas and actions that you'll find useful and reasonable.

- ✓ **You're an educator in need of ideas for helping parents or guardians of your students.** Many of the descriptions and recommendations in this book are useful for parents and educators. Just because the book was written "for parents" doesn't mean educators can't find plenty of ideas, too.

# Icons Used in This Book

Throughout this book, icons in the margins cue you in on different types of information that call out for your attention. Here are the icons you'll see and a brief description of each.

I want you to remember everything you read in this book, but if you can't quite do that, then remember the important points flagged with this icon.

Tips provide insider insight. When you're looking for helpful hints, check out these tips.

Activities suggest strategies for helping your children practice skills outside of the classroom.

# Where to Go from Here

You can approach this book in a number of ways. Reading from cover to cover provides you with a great overview of each part of the standards and with ways you can support your child's education, while picking and choosing chapters is an efficient way to get ideas and information quickly.

If you want a basic overview of the development of the standards and how they're organized, check out Chapters 1 and 2. You'll find useful ideas for creating a home environment conducive to education and connecting with your child's teachers in Chapters 3 and 4. If you're looking for a summary of the skills and concepts contained in the Common Core Standards, check out Chapters 5 and 6 for math and Chapters 7, 8, and 9 for English language arts and literacy. Part III of this book, the Part of Tens, provides you with "top ten" lists of helpful ideas and answers to common questions.

# Beyond the Book

In addition to the ideas, information, and resources provided in this book, you can access a free Cheat Sheet online at www.dummies.com/cheatsheet/commoncorestandards that contains even more suggestions for parents on the Common Core Standards.

# Part I

# Getting Up to Speed on Common Core Standards

getting started
with

Common Core

Visit www.dummies.com for free content that helps you learn more and do more.

## *In this part. . .*

✔ Get filled in about the history of the Common Core Standards and how they are being implemented.

✔ Review how the standards are organized and check out some of the major features of the math, English language arts, and literacy standards.

✔ Take a look at some ideas for supporting your child's efforts to master the standards at home.

✔ Gather some strategies for communicating and working with your child's teacher.

# Chapter 1

# Exploring Common Core's Roots

*A*s I write this chapter, 45 states and the District of Columbia are in the process of implementing the Common Core Standards, representing one of the most widespread education reform movements in the history of public education in the United States. As a parent, you probably have lots of questions about these standards, including what they are, why they're important, and what impact they're likely to have on teachers and students. These questions are at the center of a growing discussion about education in the United States. As more states enter the final stages of implementation and more schools send home information about the Common Core Standards, more and more parents have unanswered questions.

In this chapter, I field some of those general questions. I explain the motivation and purpose for developing the Common Core Standards, discuss their history from birth to the present, and discuss how states are progressing in adopting the standards and implementing them in schools. With this background information at hand, you have a much better understanding of what the standards are, why they're being adopted, and where to go from here. This chapter prepares you for a more thorough discussion, in subsequent chapters, of what's in the standards and what you can do, as a parent, to help your child or teen achieve the standards.

# Understanding the Rationale

The first question you may have is, "Why do we need new standards to begin with?" Year after year, studies show that a vast majority of students are ill-prepared academically to move on to college or secure employment with businesses that require a highly skilled workforce.

The motivation behind the development of the Common Core Standards is grounded in the idea that higher academic standards in schools, from kindergarten through high school, are likely to produce students who are better prepared to take on the challenges of a post-secondary education or a challenging and rewarding career directly out of high school.

## Recognizing the standards

The Common Core Standards set consistent and clear expectations for what students must know at the completion of each grade from kindergarten through high school. The standards establish expectations in three academic areas:

- ✓ **Mathematics:** The Common Core Standards for mathematics focus on gaining essential understanding to help students acquire a deeper knowledge of only the most important concepts and develop the skills to tackle mathematical problems in the real world. The standards call on students to develop deeper knowledge and higher-level skills in each successive grade, so it's vitally important that students get a handle on the material covered in each grade before advancing to a higher grade level.

- ✓ **English language arts (ELA):** The ELA standards are structured to build foundational literacy skills in early grades and to continue to equip students with reading and writing skills as they progress into middle and high school. The standards gradually increase in complexity from grade to grade, so pay special attention to the additional concepts and skills added from one grade to the next.

✔ **Literacy:** The literacy standards establish reading and writing expectations for students in social studies, science, and technology. These standards provide few specifics on *what* students need to read or write, focusing instead on *how* students should read and write in these courses and how to evaluate what qualifies as good writing.

## Recognizing the goals

The Common Core Standards address the shortcomings and build upon the strengths of current state standards. Governors, education officials, and educators who developed the Common Core Standards had several goals in mind, including the following:

✔ **Raise the bar for students in Grades K–12.** Higher academic standards represent higher expectations for student learning. Higher rigor and demand in classrooms increase the likelihood that more students will master essential skills and concepts in math, reading, and writing that will prepare them for success when they move to the next grade or course or on to college or a career.

✔ **Clarify expectations for students, teachers, and parents.** Inconsistent, complicated standards are difficult for everyone to understand and follow, from school administrators and teachers to parents and students. Common Core Standards are intended to be consistent and clear, so everyone involved in the learning process can collaborate on meeting expectations.

As you find out more about Common Core Standards, you're likely to hear the phrase "fewer, clearer, and higher" used to describe the first two goals on this list.

✔ **Standardize benchmarks for academic achievement across all 50 states.** Major discrepancies in the expectations of student performance from state to state make it difficult to determine which states are doing the best job of preparing students for college or career. Having the same benchmarks for students across state lines helps ensure that students from different states are being held to similar standards of academic achievement.

# Higher standards or not?

Critics of the Common Core Standards believe that the standards are less rigorous than the current standards in some states and also fail to meet the benchmarks set by some international education systems. However, a study conducted by the Thomas B. Fordham Institute in 2010, "The State of State Standards," found that the Common Core Standards for mathematics were more rigorous than the standards in 39 states. The remaining states had standards in mathematics similar in rigor to the Common Core Standards. The same report found that only California, Indiana, and the District of Columbia had English language arts standards that were more demanding than the Common Core Standards.

✓ **Ensure that all students are prepared for college or career.** One of the fundamental goals of all schools is preparing students to pursue their goals after they graduate from high school, whether they enter college or the workforce. This isn't something that just happens in Grade 12 or even in high school. College and career readiness is the outcome of an effective education in kindergarten through Grade 12. This is why higher, more-consistent standards are important at all grade levels.

✓ **Communicate real-world expectations.** Connecting what students are asked to do in school to the demands of the real world is a difficult job, but it's vital to making sure that students understand what's required of them when they go to college or get a job. The skills and concepts taught in schools need to be the same skills and concepts students use in higher learning or the job market.

Without high academic standards that outline the knowledge and skills students need in math, English, and reading and writing in other subjects, few students are ready to tackle college or a career after they graduate from high school.

# Tracing Common Core's History

The push for common standards shared by multiple states isn't new. Conversations about "common" or "national" standards have been a significant part of the public discussion on education for several decades. However, efforts to agree on a common set of standards for state departments of education and, as a result, local school districts have often been sidetracked by concerns that the federal government would become overly involved.

In the following sections, I describe the hurdles and the history of attempts to standardize measures of academic achievement.

## Identifying the barriers

Efforts under the administrations of President George H. W. Bush and President Bill Clinton to establish common standards among the states failed because of a few key issues:

- ✔ **State leaders want to retain oversight.** In general, each state has a department of education, although the name sometimes varies from state to state. Among other things, the departments of education oversee education policy, administer statewide assessments, distribute federal and state funding, and monitor compliance with state and federal laws. State lawmakers, policymakers, and leaders oversee a majority of the decisions relating to education. Differences of opinion over what's best for students and a desire to remain competitive with other states have made agreeing on national reforms very difficult.

- ✔ **Educators want to maintain local control over curriculum.** Some teachers and parents feel threatened by standards because they see standards as the government's attempt to dictate curriculum. They don't realize that standards dictate only what students need to know upon completion of each grade level. Curriculum choices, including which materials are used to teach certain subjects in each grade, are still left up to schools and districts. However, fears of government overreach are still a barrier for some people.

As I explain in Chapter 2, Common Core Standards don't dictate *curriculum* — how teachers teach and the specific materials they use to help their students meet the expectations outlined by the standards. The standards establish expectations for what students know and are able to do academically at different grade levels.

✔ **Reaching consensus is difficult.** National leaders find it easier to agree that all students should be proficient in reading than to reach a consensus on what they should read. The same is true in other subject areas. Tensions over nailing down the specifics of what should be taught nationwide have been a major contributing factor to the failure of previous education-reform efforts. For the most part, Common Core clears this hurdle by focusing on what students should know and not how they come to know it.

Recognizing these barriers, you can better understand why the discussion of standards common to all states raises concerns. In the 1990s, several efforts to rally support for common standards were put on hold because of fears that local control would be compromised. Who decides what goes in the standards? What materials will be used to teach? When is a student supposed to know certain material and master certain skills? Differences of opinion over the answers to these questions represent some of the reasons that previous efforts to develop common standards were unsuccessful.

## Resuming the conversation

The No Child Left Behind Act of 2001 reignited the discussion about common standards. Signed into law by President George W. Bush in January 2002, No Child Left Behind increased state accountability, among other criteria, for reaching certain levels of educational attainment and reporting those outcomes. Although the emphasis was on increasing the level of state accountability for student progress, certain components of No Child Left Behind sparked renewed interest in common standards:

✔ **Focusing on student progress:** Every school in every state was required to meet certain achievement targets on assessments that measure student learning in math and English, with further specifications for certain demographic groups. Called "adequate yearly progress" (AYP), these benchmarks became the measures by which schools, districts, and states were graded on their ability to educate students. Consequently, an emphasis on measuring student progress was accompanied by an intensified focus on exactly what was being measured.

✔ **Accentuating the disconnect between states:** No Child Left Behind presented a significant challenge that involved the measurement of student progress with AYP, which compared progress in each state. The difficulty was that each state used its own standards for learning and for determining proficiency in subjects. The result? Some states had remarkably high proficiency rates in math and English, while others were considerably lower.

✔ **Learning from national assessments:** According to the National Assessment of Educational Progress (NAEP), an annual test that measures performance across core academic subject areas in each state, certain states consistently outperform other states in math, reading, writing, science, history, the arts, and other assessed areas. The assessments used by individual states didn't reflect the same distribution of scores.

After looking at only a few years of test scores from states using different standards and tests, educators and legislators concluded that, without common standards, comparing student achievement between states would be next to impossible. A comparison of NAEP scores to the results of individual state assessments reinforces this fact. These considerations have persuaded more and more state leaders and policymakers to pursue common standards once again. Their goal: to introduce a degree of consistency and clarity regarding educational expectations across state lines.

# Developing the Common Core Standards

With renewed purpose, state leaders and policymakers confronted the issue of common standards again in 2006. After policymakers took a closer look at the differences in content and rigor among the states' standards, investigated the influence of high standards in other countries, and gathered feedback on implementing the standards, the move toward common standards was in full swing.

The two organizations that officially led the development of the Common Core Standards were the National Governors Association Center for Best Practices and the Council of Chief State School Officers. In early 2009, a meeting of state education leaders in Chicago resulted in overwhelming support for the idea of common standards. By the summer of 2009, all but two states, Texas and Alaska, had signed an agreement to participate in the development of the Common Core Standards.

## Meeting the Common Core architects

Although the final draft of Common Core Standards represents input from educators, state leaders, policymakers, parents, and others who participated in the process of submitting public feedback, two individuals most often labeled the "architects" of the Common Core Standards are David Coleman and Jason Zimba. For the National Governors Association Center for Best Practices and the Council of Chief State School Officers, these two were a natural fit to lead the process of standards writing because of a report they produced in 2007 that called for "fewer, clearer, and higher" academic standards in math and science.

The process of writing the Common Core Standards began in 2009 and involved consulting existing state standards, researching college and career readiness, and exploring international education systems. The public was able to comment on a first draft of the standards released in September 2009, followed by a second draft for comment in March 2010. After nearly 10,000 individuals provided input on the standards, a final draft was released in June 2010. After years of trying to agree on common standards for states, the Common Core Standards were ready for adoption.

# State Adoptions and Implementation

At the same time that the Common Core Standards were written, President Barack Obama announced a competitive grant program called Race to the Top, offering more than $4 billion in available funds. The grant sought to provide federal funding for education reform at the state level. Among other criteria, the opportunity to receive a slice of this pie required states to revamp their academic standards. This included pursuing common standards backed by college and career readiness research with other states. Although states didn't necessarily have to adopt the Common Core Standards to be eligible for the grant, the fact that 48 states had agreed to contribute to the development of the standards certainly made them a viable option.

The process for adopting academic standards varies from state to state. In general, some combination of the state legislature, a body empowered by the state legislature or governor (such as a state board of education), and the state department of education is responsible for recommending and approving standards for use by schools and districts. As the Common Core Standards neared completion in 2010, conversations regarding adoption took place in a majority of states.

## Recognizing Common Core states

Most states adopted the Common Core Standards between 2010 and 2012. A majority of adopting states did so in 2010 to meet the timelines and specifications for common standards in the Race to the Top grant. However, not all states considering adoption of common standards took the same path. In fact, states pursued a few different options:

✔ **Adopting the standards verbatim:** Verbatim adoption of the Common Core Standards means that a state adopts the Common Core Standards for mathematics, English language arts, and literacy without adding to or taking away any content. The standards for mathematics and English language arts provide learning expectations for those subjects, while the literacy standards set expectations for reading and writing skills for social studies, science, and technology.

✔ **Adding 15 percent:** States that adopt the Common Core Standards have the option to add 15 percent to the total number of standards in a specific subject area. A state can decide to do this if adding content in certain grades or courses, or on certain subjects, is necessary. However, adopting states can't choose to remove standards from the Common Core.

✔ **Deciding to go it alone:** In order to qualify for the Race to the Top grant, states didn't have to adopt the Common Core Standards. States had the option of developing and adopting common standards in conjunction with other states. With that option in place, some states opted to take alternative paths.

For information on what your state chose to do, check out your state's website. You can also visit www.corestandards.org.

## Striving to implement Common Core

Implementation of the Common Core Standards refers to the process of actually putting the standards to use in schools and districts. When it adopted the Common Core Standards, each state set a goal for when it would fully implement the standards. And because states adopted the Common Core Standards at different times, the timeline for full implementation of the standards varies by state. Regardless of the date set for a full implementation of the Common Core Standards, keep a few things in mind about the process:

✓ **Starting on the standards:** The process of implementing the standards depends on decisions made in each state. Some states may start teaching toward the standards all at once, while others may use a gradual phase-in approach. Having a good grasp on the approach being used in your state helps you better understand how to support the process at home. For more information on the approach being used in your state, reach out to your local school or district for more information.

✓ **Deciding on new books and materials:** Because the Common Core Standards establish concepts and skills that are potentially different from previous state standards, school districts are likely to use new textbooks and materials as they start teaching to the standards. Getting familiar with these resources will assist you in helping your student tackle the new standards (see Chapter 3 for details).

✓ **Developing a new assessment:** A change in standards usually triggers a change in the assessment used to measure student progress. Partnership for Assessment of Readiness for College and Careers (PARCC) is a 19-state consortium that's developing K–12 assessments that measure achievement of Common Core Standards. Visit www.parcconline.org. Another consortium is developing what it calls Smarter Balanced Assessments; for more information, visit www.smarterbalanced.org.

# Chapter 2

# Grasping the Basics of the Common Core Standards

* * * * * * * * * * * * * * * * * * * * * * * * * * * * * * * * * * * * *

*In This Chapter*

▶ Taking on the math practices and standards

▶ Exploring the English language arts and literacy standards

▶ Reviewing the shifts in classroom instruction

* * * * * * * * * * * * * * * * * * * * * * * * * * * * * * * * * * * * *

*T*he Common Core Standards are divided into two major subjects: mathematics and English language arts (ELA). Each of these subjects contains content standards for kindergarten through Grade 12. These standards outline the expectations for what students should master by the end of each grade level in mathematics and English language arts.

The English language arts standards include a section of literacy standards for history, social studies, science, and technical subjects. These standards apply to Grades 6–12 and include expectations for reading and writing skills in those subject areas and others.

To help your child meet the expectations established by the Common Core Standards, you need to know what the standards are and how they're organized. This enables you to quickly look up the grade-specific standards that apply to your child and find any resources available to help your child achieve the standards.

In this chapter, I introduce the math and ELA standards, describe how they're organized, and describe each of the key standards in a nutshell. I wrap up this chapter with an explanation of the instructional shifts you may encounter as your school system implements Common Core.

## Getting your hands on the standards

The Common Core Standards contain far more detail than I can cover in this relatively short book and more detail than you need to get started. However, if you want more specifics about a particular standard, you can access it online.

To obtain a copy of the Common Core Standards and appendixes, visit `www.corestandards.org`. You can also print a hard copy of the standards and appendixes from this website. I encourage you to use the printable versions of the standards. This format presents details in a much more accessible format, with charts and tables that are excellent for quick reference.

If you live in a state that has adopted the Common Core Standards, you should also check with your department of education's website. Because adopting states can add up to 15 percent more content to the standards, you want the most complete and accurate version for your state.

# Brushing Up on Mathematics Practice and Content Standards

The Common Core Standards for Mathematical Practice are composed of the following three key components:

✔ **Standards for mathematical practice:** These standards outline ways of thinking about math and approaching problems that help to develop students' thinking skills. The practice standards stress understanding over procedures; for example, students are expected not only to solve the equation $2 + 2 = 4$ but also to recognize situations calling for addition and to apply that understanding to real life.

The practice standards apply to all math concepts and skills at all grade levels. See "Meeting the Standards for mathematical practice" later in this chapter for details.

✔ **Content standards:** Using the lens of the mathematical practices, the content standards focus on more specific math concepts and skills that students are expected to know and encounter in each area of math at each grade level. Content standards are organized in the following two ways:

- **By grade level:** For Grades K–8, content standards are organized by grade level. For high school, content standards are organized by subject, such as algebra, geometry, and statistics and probability.

- **By domain:** *Domains* are groups of concepts and skills, such as operations and algebraic thinking, that can be found within all grade levels. These categories help you see how a particular concept progresses in difficulty from grade to grade.

✔ **Mathematics appendix:** Titled "Designing High School Mathematics Courses Based on the Common Core State Standards," the resources in this appendix provide school administrators and math teachers with options for developing courses to help students achieve Common Core math principles and standards in high school.

In the following sections, I explain practice and content standards in greater detail and describe what's included in the appendix to the math standards.

## Meeting the standards for mathematical practice

The Standards for Mathematical Practice stress the importance of developing a conceptual understanding of various mathematical principles and being able to apply mathematical knowledge and skills to solve problems.

In other words, practice standards set the bar for how well students are able to apply their mathematical knowledge and skills to solve problems and understand what they're doing and why. Think of practice standards in terms of a doctor not only being able to pass a test but also being able to use that same knowledge to accurately diagnose medical conditions and effectively treat patients. The practice standards set expectations that students at all levels master the following habits of mind as they apply to the content standards at each student's grade level:

✔ **Understand mathematical problems and persist in solving them.** Students need to have a clear understanding of what they're required to do in math problems and why they're supposed to do it. Acquiring this skill involves students asking questions as they work through problems and continually self-monitoring to make sure they understand why they're taking certain steps.

✔ **Think about different aspects of a problem as separate and related parts.** Sometimes students need to think about what something means apart from the rest of the problem. In math, this means they understand not only the operations needed to solve specific parts of a problem but also how to break down the problem to use different operations to successfully solve the entire problem.

✔ **Understand a concept well enough to explain and defend an answer.** Solving a problem correctly is great, but having the know-how to get the correct answer and then explain and defend how you got it is even better. When students can verbalize their thought process in a way that gives support to the steps they took to solve a problem, question the thought processes of others to decide whether they make sense, and ask useful questions to better understand a problem, then you have a good indication that they truly understand the concept.

✔ **Apply understanding of a concept to a real-life situation.** We've probably all had the experience of sitting in a math class and wondering when we were ever going to use the information being presented. A major step toward mastery of any concept involves understanding the applications of that concept to real life. Successfully relating math concepts to real-life situations shows that a student can transfer an isolated skill to a broad realm of possibilities. The more a student practices this skill, the more connections he is likely to see for applying it to real-world situations.

✔ **Choose the right resources to help solve problems.** When working a math problem, students usually have a variety of resources to help them solve the problem, including calculators, graphs, rulers, and scratch paper. The standards also stress the use of concrete models, digital content, and mathematical software. Knowing when and how to pick the right resources to solve a particular math problem is an indication of how well students actually understand the problem they're solving. Efficiently solving problems with the proper tools is a better indication of mastery than trial and error.

✔ **Pay attention to the details.** The world of mathematics rewards specificity. The better students become at using math-specific vocabulary and calculating efficiently and accurately to the degree of precision required by the situation, the sooner they gain proficiency and fluidity when solving problems. Math requires students to keep track of the details in order to be successful problem solvers.

✔ **Find and use patterns in problems.** As students get more comfortable with certain math concepts, they begin to pick up on patterns and structures that enable them to break apart problems with greater ease. Many younger children do this naturally when they sort and order manipulative objects such as blocks, but this habit of mind can require some practice as students move into more complex math.

This skill comes with lots of practice. Isolating a certain part of the problem to make better sense of the whole is an effective skill in math. Being able to do it repeatedly in various contexts indicates that a student can see patterns and successfully use them to his advantage.

✔ **Look for and use repeated reasoning.** Understanding that some steps or procedures are repetitive saves students a considerable amount of time. When students grasp this skill, they're able to circumvent repetitive processes and quickly move on to solve the problem. However, arriving at a place of familiarity that allows students to recognize processes that repeat takes practice and an eye for detail.

With any mathematical concept the standards introduce, any number of math practice standards come into play along with the content standards. Keep in mind that the Standards for Mathematical Practice are used on a case-by-case basis depending on which math content standards your child is learning and the specific problem your child is trying to solve.

# Digging deeper into the math practices

To view detailed descriptions of the Common Core Standards for Mathematical Practice and the math content standards, visit www.corestandards.org. The process standards outlined by the National Council of Teachers of Mathematics and the proficiency standards determined by the National Research Council served as significant resources in the development of the practice standards. For more information on either of these resources, visit www.nctm.org and www.nationalacademies.org.

# Getting familiar with content standards by domain

The Common Core content standards for mathematics are all part of specific domains, or categories, that are often relevant to multiple grade levels, for example, students work on operations and algebraic thinking from kindergarten through Grade 5, as I explain in Chapter 5. The idea behind this approach is that certain concepts in math progress in complexity over several years.

The following sections introduce and describe the domains that apply in kindergarten through Grade 8. Some of these domains are also addressed in high school, but at a much more complex level. Chapter 6 contains specific details on the requirements of the high-school standards. The following sections, with descriptions of the domains and grade levels, provide basic overviews of some of the skills and concepts for which students are expected to demonstrate proficiency for each domain. (For grade-specific information on Common Core math standards, see Chapters 5 and 6.)

## Counting and cardinality

Counting and cardinality involves getting comfortable with what numbers represent and how they're used. Students count numbers 1 to 100, work on writing numbers 1 to 20, and solidify their understanding of numbers as representative of the total quantity of objects in a group.

You may also see this domain referenced as developing "number sense." Counting and cardinality is the first step in a conceptual staircase of mathematics that students climb over the course of their school years.

## Operations and algebraic thinking

The primary emphasis in the operations and algebraic thinking domain (Grades K–5) is to develop comfort and fluency when using numbers to add, subtract, multiply, and divide. Numbers emerge as tools that students can use to identify and represent quantities, relationships, and patterns. Starting with understanding how to take apart and put together numbers within 10 and understanding relationships between parts and wholes, students build upon these skills until they're comfortable with multiplying and dividing up to 100, adding and subtracting decimals fluently, and multiplying and dividing decimals to the hundredths place.

This leads to the application of these skills in finding missing parts, solving problems with multiple steps, finding the solution to numerical expressions, and using these concepts to determine patterns and represent data on a coordinate plane.

### Number and operations in base ten

This domain (Grades K–5) stresses *place value* — the value of a digit according to its position in a number (for example, in the number 346, the 4 represents 40). Over the course of these grades, students gain an understanding of the use and function of numbers, place value with whole numbers, and eventually place value with multidigit numbers and decimals.

Over several grades, students tackle the idea that place value for each digit, to the right or the left of the decimal, is 10 times more than and $\frac{1}{10}$ as much as the digit beside it.

### Number and operations — fractions

Fractions (Grades 3–5) can be challenging for many students, especially after getting comfortable with whole numbers in earlier grades. The standards in this domain are designed to help students see fractions *as* numbers, or more specifically as parts of a whole, instead of as foreign symbols that are difficult to comprehend. Students explore the relationship of parts to wholes; the notation involved in expressing fractions; the ordering of fractions based on their values; and the use of fractions in addition, in subtraction, and in limited applications of multiplication and division.

### Measurement and data

In early grades (Grades K–5), students explore measurement and data by measuring objects and quantities and telling time as a means of collecting data. This undergirds the central understanding that numbers may be used as a means of classification based on quantity. With this concept under their belts, students begin to perform other operations, such as addition and subtraction, using gathered data. Geometric concepts and shapes are also introduced as a part of this domain. High-school students pursue the use of data more extensively with an emphasis on statistics and probability.

### Geometry

Starting with a basic understanding of shapes in kindergarten, students explore properties of shapes and other geometric concepts in later grades. As students proceed through Grades

5–8 and into high school, they begin to focus on the application of geometry to real-world settings.

## Ratios and proportional relationships

In Grades 6–7, students strive to gain mastery of ratios and proportions. With a firm understanding of the basic tenets of multiplication and division, students explore relationships between sets of numbers and use mathematical terms to describe any relationships that exist. Significant emphasis is placed on real-world application. Students dig into proportions and unit rates — for example, the proportional relationship of the cost of goods and services or the distance traveled over a certain period of time at a given speed.

## The number system

Students extend their abilities in addition, subtraction, multiplication, and division in Grades 6–8 as they apply these operations to multidigit whole numbers and to fractions. The concept of rational and irrational numbers (numbers that can or can't be written as a fraction or ratio of two whole numbers) is also a component of these grades. Students continue to graph data and closed figures in a coordinate plane and use their results to make determinations for specific problems.

## Expressions and equations

In Grades 6–8, students apply their understanding of basic arithmetic and part/whole reasoning to solve algebraic expressions, discovering how to substitute letters for numbers and solve to find unknown values. Students then begin to compare various expressions to find out whether they're equivalent. Teachers introduce students to the idea of using exponents to denote significantly large or small numbers and show them how to solve linear equations and graph them in a coordinate plane. (*Linear equations* appear as a straight line when drawn on a grid; they form a pattern that can be expressed using a linear equation.)

## Functions

Understanding relationships between numbers and relationships between ratios is an essential aspect of Grade 8. Students must know what a *function* is: a rule, equation, or expression that produces only one output for every input. For example, height is generally a function of age, because the older you are, the taller you get (to a certain point). If you measure your height on your birthday every year, your data set includes only one height for every birthday.

Students must also be able to display functions in various ways — with words, graphs, or numbers, for example. As they progress in their ability to recognize and use functions in Grade 8 and in high school, students are required to use functions to show the relationship between objects in real life — for example, how fast something changes or grows over time.

### Statistics and probability

Students dive into statistics and probability in Grades 6–8 and again in high school. They explore basic concepts of variability first so they can get a handle on the fact that data (such as age, height, or weight) varies from person to person. They also practice displaying sets of data in various forms.

After grasping the basics, students apply their understanding to make determinations about larger populations based on data samples. Students eventually use graphs, scatterplots, and tables to represent multiple forms of data that may include more than one variable.

### Domains in high school

The high-school content standards are grouped within six domains: number and quantity, algebra, functions, modeling, geometry, and statistics and probability. Some of these domains (functions, geometry, and statistics and probability) are extensions of domains that are addressed in lower grades. The rest are new domains that build on previously learned concepts. For more information on the specific content outlined by the high-school standards, see Chapter 6.

## Looking at the mathematics appendix

The appendix to the Common Core Standards for Mathematical Practice outlines some ideas on how to organize the math standards into courses in high school. Although these decisions will probably be made by your child's school or district, it's important for you to know the available options.

High schools can organize their math courses in two basic ways:

- ✔ **Traditional:** You're probably familiar with the traditional pathway for math courses in high school, which consists of courses like algebra, geometry, and so on.

- ✔ **Integrated:** This pathway integrates standards from the various domains into Math I, II, and III. Each course has a different area of emphasis but includes skills and concepts from multiple domains.

Other resources in this appendix outline ideas and options for accelerated course pathways, including suggestions for ways to challenge students who are successful in math and need opportunities to engage with more complex math.

 If you have questions about the organization of your child's math courses, contact an administrator or math teacher at your local school or district.

# Exploring the English Language Arts Standards

The Common Core Standards for English Language Arts and Literacy in History/Social Studies, Science, and Technical Subjects are composed of the following three key components:

- ✔ **ELA grade-level standards for K–12:** The ELA grade-level standards set expectations for students in reading, writing, speaking, listening, and language. These standards are organized in two ways:

  - • **By anchor standards:** The College and Career Readiness (CCR) Anchor Standards set broad expectations for what students should know upon graduation from high school in each of the ELA domains: reading, writing, speaking and listening, and language. These standards outline the central concepts addressed in each domain without the grade-level specifics.

  - • **By domain and grade level:** ELA standards are presented first by domain and then by grade level within the domain. The ELA domains for reading are literature, informational text, and foundational skills. The ELA domains for writing are speaking and listening, and language. To look up standards for a specific grade level, go to the domain first and then the grade level within that domain.

- **By text complexity:** A final component of each domain is the "range, quality, and complexity" of texts used to accomplish the skills in each domain.

✔ **Grades 6–12 literacy standards:** The literacy standards apply to Grades 6–12 in history, social studies, science, and technical subjects, and very likely to any subject areas not specifically mentioned. Common Core Standards for literacy are presented in three categories:

- History/social studies

- Science and technical subjects

- Writing

Within each of these domains, standards are divided not by individual grades but by three grade bands: Grades 6–8, 9–10, and 11–12. These standards are listed side by side in the paper version so you can easily see how they progress in difficulty from one grade band to the next.

Separate reading standards are provided for social studies and for science and technical subjects. One set of writing standards addresses skills for writing in all of these subjects.

✔ **ELA appendixes:** The ELA standards include three appendixes (Appendix A, B, and C), each containing background material and resources you may find useful. See "Tapping the ELA appendixes for more info," later in this chapter.

## Improving reading comprehension

The Common Core reading standards range from kindergarten through Grade 12 and are used with any genres students encounter in English and reading classes. These standards are designed to guide students over time to a place of reading proficiency and a state of reading preparedness (experience with a wide variety of text types) that is fitting for college or career. It is of vital importance to keep up with your child's progress in mastering the reading standards as he moves from one grade to the next. The easiest way to do this is to keep a copy of the standards close at hand and to make a note when your child finds a particular standard to be challenging. If, even with your support, he can't master a particular standard, take the opportunity to reach out to the teacher for assistance.

The reading standards are divided into three separate categories:

✔ **Literature:** These standards emphasize the central skills and details that are vital to your child's success in reading fictional literature in kindergarten through Grade 12, such as analyzing characters, determining the meaning or message of a piece of literature, and analyzing an author's purpose.

✔ **Informational text:** Standards in this category highlight essential components of successful and meaningful reading experiences with informational, nonfiction texts in kindergarten through Grade 12. Citing evidence to support ideas, using vocabulary correctly, and analyzing the structure and purpose of an author's writings are all important components of the informational-text standards.

✔ **Foundational skills:** In kindergarten through Grade 5, the foundational skills standards are designed to bolster students' reading abilities. Basic skills and concepts related to topics such as syllables, phonics, and reading fluency and comprehension are outlined in the standards.

# Balancing fiction and nonfiction

The Common Core Standards call for an appropriate balance between reading fiction and nonfiction as students move from grade to grade. The standards are designed to support instruction that consists of a 50/50 balance between nonfiction and fiction by Grade 4, with the emphasis shifting to 70 percent nonfiction in high school.

Note that these percentages account for the entire slate of reading materials that a student encounters during the school year, including in science and social studies. It's safe to assume that a significant majority of time spent reading in English classes will include fictional literature. On the other hand, a majority of reading materials in science and social studies classes will most likely be nonfiction, resulting in the appropriate balance between fiction and nonfiction.

# Honing writing skills

The writing standards, which apply to kindergarten through Grade 12, are designed to ensure that your child's mastery of writing progresses with each school year. As with the reading standards, many of the writing standards seek to develop writers who pay close attention to details within source texts and can use evidence to support their claims or thoughts. The writing standards also require that students use proper style in writing and make use of structure when crafting a piece of writing. Three types of writing play a central role in these standards:

- **Argumentative or persuasive writing:** This style of writing forces students to state a claim and provide evidence to back it up. Students are expected to clearly use well-reasoned arguments or other persuasive methods to convince their readers of the central point(s) being conveyed.

- **Expository or informational writing:** Expository writing calls for students to explain or inform readers regarding a specific topic or task. This writing style often involves the use of various terms and definitions, illustrations, instructions, and representations.

- **Narrative writing:** As a separate and distinct style, narrative writing is only applicable to English classes and fiction writing. Students assume the role of narrator as they tell stories or relate sequences of events. Narrative writing involves scenes, settings, and characters. However, in classes where nonfiction writing is required, such as science or social studies, this style of writing often involves describing occurrences, such as historical events or scientific processes, placing emphasis on cause and effect. These writing skills are addressed in the literacy standards in Grades 6–12, where narrative writing is included in argumentative and informative writing, and not treated as a separate style.

# Cultivating speaking and listening skills

To be successful in their personal, academic, and professional lives, students must be able to listen and understand as information is provided in different mediums, including spoken words, images, and videos. They must also be able to express themselves and their ideas clearly in speech and through multimedia presentations. The speaking and listening domain sets expectations for students in these areas.

From kindergarten through Grade 12, students participate in increasingly complex presentations. In lower grades, this includes consenting to and following rules for discussion in class and expressing ideas in a clear and understandable fashion. In later grades, students collaborate to set their own norms for discussion and present results from writing and research using various mediums, including audio, video, and slide-show presentations.

Reinforce speaking and listening skills at home early and often. If your child has trouble understanding what you tell her, consider having her repeat what you said in her own words. This challenges her to not only listen carefully but also to formulate clear and concise expressions. See Chapters 7 to 9 for additional ideas on how to reinforce speaking and listening skills at home.

## Fine-tuning grammar, usage, mechanics, and vocabulary

Students dig into the nuts and bolts of the English language in kindergarten through Grade 12. In lower grades, students tackle the basics of spelling and writing, including forming letters properly, writing complete sentences, and properly using other grammatical conventions. As they move into the middle and upper grades, students encounter increasingly complex aspects of language, such as the use of various forms and styles of writing and specialized vocabulary.

## Addressing Standard 10

Standard 10: Range, Quality, and Complexity serves as a bookend for the reading and writing skills developed in kindergarten through Grade 12. While striving to attain the reading and writing standards, students encounter and make use of a significant number of texts. To ensure the use of proper texts, Standard 10 draws attention to complexity, quality, and types of texts used across grade levels. Standard 10 sets the following guidelines for text selection:

✔ **Range: Various forms of fictional literature and informational text are to be used across grade levels.** Because fictional and informational texts play an important role in the standards, the standards offer guidance on the types of texts in each category that are appropriate for use. In fictional literature, this includes poetry, short stories, and novels. For informational text, charts, maps, autobiographies and biographies, and speeches are examples of recommended sources.

✔ **Quality: Consult the standards for guidance on texts that reflect appropriate readings.** Although the decision about what students will read is ultimately up to teachers, schools, and districts, the standards include recommendations for texts that are representative of the quality of reading materials appropriate for each grade level. You'll find these very helpful as you look for ways to support and enhance your child's reading skills.

✔ **Complexity: Texts should reflect an appropriate complexity for the subject and the reader.** Students struggle to read for information when a text is too complex. Text complexity is measured by several factors, including the *Lexile level* (a quantitative measurement that scores a text based on the complexity of the language and sentence structure). The standards give guidance on appropriate levels of text complexity for certain grades, subjects, and ability levels.

## The literacy standards

In Grades 6–12, the reading and writing standards in history, social studies, science, and technical subjects are separated from English language arts standards. The reading standards are divided into two sections, one for each of the following:

✔ History and social studies

✔ Science and technical subjects

One set of writing standards sets the bar for writing in all three subjects. The literacy standards are covered in just a few pages, so they're easy to use as a quick reference when reading and writing in these subjects.

### History and social studies

The reading standards for history and social studies focus heavily on the use and analysis of primary and secondary sources. Students determine the central idea(s), cite evidence to support conclusions, and analyze the structure of writings and an author's purpose in writing. Each of these skills is then utilized when students begin to write for the purposes of conveying information or arguing a particular position.

Because the reading standards are designed for use alongside other subjects (to facilitate the fluent reading of documents that are central to the subject being studied), the skills should be viewed as tools that enable students to access deeper levels of knowledge and to convey ideas through structured and well-reasoned writings.

### Science and technical subjects

The reading standards for science and technical subjects are geared for use with texts that explain processes and procedures or involve information presented in the form of data or other mediums. Students primarily work to find meaning in these texts and compare the information contained in multiple sources.

The writing standards for these subjects are the same as those used in history and social studies, but students direct their efforts toward the integration of the knowledge and ideas garnered from their reading of informational texts.

## Tapping the ELA appendixes

The appendixes to the English language arts standards include a variety of resources that are useful for parents and educators. Unlike the appendix to the math standards, which only addresses the upper grades, these appendixes include materials applicable to all grades:

- ✔ **Appendix A focuses on text complexity and the research behind the standards.** Check out this section for more information on how to evaluate a text's complexity and whether it's appropriate for your child. Appendix A also reviews some of the research behind the standards and their use.

- ✔ **Appendix B contains examples of appropriate texts for each grade level and samples of student tasks.** Consult this appendix for ideas on texts that are representative of the desired complexity for each grade level. You'll find recommendations for literature, history, science, and other subjects. Another helpful aspect of this appendix is the inclusion of sample tasks. These tasks give you a better idea of what your child will be asked to do with the material she's reading.

✔ **Appendix C includes samples of student writing aligned to the literacy standards.** Take a look at this appendix to see some actual examples of student work with feedback on how well each piece of writing aligns to the expectations of the standards. These examples are particularly helpful in assessing your child's performance and progress.

As a parent, you're likely to find Appendix B the most useful of the three because it contains sample reading passages and tasks for students to perform. Appendix C is also useful because it contains a collection of student writing along with notes to help you distinguish good writing from not-so-good

# Differentiating standards from curriculum

Before you dive deeper into the standards, I want to clarify the difference between the Common Core Standards covered in this book and the curriculum that your child's teacher uses in her classroom:

✔ **Standards** delineate the skills and concepts that a student is expected to master by the end of a particular grade level — for example, being able to divide fractions or to identify the prepositions in a sentence.

✔ **Curriculum** is made up of the materials and resources that a teacher uses to teach the standards. For example, a teacher

may use a selection from *To Kill a Mockingbird* by Harper Lee to teach about symbolism in literature. Or a teacher may use an example from an investment company to teach the concept of interest.

Even though the standards list some recommendations for texts that are appropriate for certain grade levels, they're only recommendations. The standards require very few specific texts. By and large, states choose standards, but decisions regarding curriculum are left up to administrators, teachers, and school boards.

writing. Appendix A goes more into the rationale behind using various measures of text complexity and the research related to the standards — something of greater interest to educators.

# Focusing on Instructional Shifts

Although the Common Core Standards don't dictate curriculum, changes in expectations for what students need to know and be able to do call for changes in the ways various skills and concepts are taught. The nature of the organization and structure of the Common Core Standards actually opens the door to a few key instructional shifts that you may notice as your child moves from grade to grade.

Student Achievement Partners, an organization founded by some of the lead writers of the Common Core Standards, has identified several key instructional shifts in both math and ELA, which I summarize in the following sections. For more information on these instructional shifts and Student Achievement Partners, visit www.achievethecore.org.

## Navigating instructional shifts in math

Instructional shifts in math center on improving essential skills, deepening understanding of concepts, and making math relevant to real-world situations:

- ✔ **Focusing on essential skills and concepts:** The Common Core Standards are designed to be a more rigorous set of standards that allow for greater understanding because students focus on fewer skills and concepts but explore those skills and concepts at a deeper level.

- ✔ **Creating a clearer sense of structure:** The progression of skills from one grade to the next is apparent when you dig into the standards. This ensures that what a student learns in one grade will be used and built upon in the next grade.

- ✔ **Infusing rigor into practice and application:** Math isn't just about learning formulas and practicing procedures. To help students connect the dots between the theoretical and practical sides of math, the math standards include criteria that develop students' understanding of key concepts, related procedures, and areas where they can apply content to real-life situations.

# Exploring instructional shifts in English language arts and literacy

Instructional shifts for English and literacy-based subjects raise the bar for students by challenging them to read and understand more complex texts, build vocabulary, and extract details from texts to use as supporting material in essays and other written work:

- ✔ **Emphasizing important nonfiction writings:** More nonfiction and informational texts are used and are a point of emphasis in classes such as science and social studies. Literature (such as classic short stories, novels, poems, and plays) is still an important part of English and reading classes, but nonfiction plays an important role as students prepare to read texts of similar complexity to those they will encounter after they graduate from high school.

- ✔ **Citing evidence from fiction and nonfiction texts:** An emphasis on citing evidence from texts requires readers to pay close attention to details and supporting statements. Building readers who are accountable to the text and the details within the text is a key component of these standards and also makes for more effective writers.

- ✔ **Reading complex texts and building vocabulary:** Increasing reading comprehension and literacy skills requires consistent practice reading texts that are appropriately complex for the student's reading level. Vocabulary also plays a central role in this process, as a reader's ability to discern the meaning of words is a critical part of understanding a text and writing effectively when using complex texts as resources.

# Chapter 3

# Supporting Common Core at Home: Your Role as a Parent

. . . . . . . . . . . . . . . . . . . . . . . . . . . . . . . . . . . . . .

## In This Chapter

▶ Building an education-centered home

▶ Practicing lifelong learning together

▶ Cultivating curiosity and critical thinking

▶ Providing educational resources to feed a hungry mind

▶ Connecting education to the real world

. . . . . . . . . . . . . . . . . . . . . . . . . . . . . . . . . . . . . .

*T*he fact that you are reading this book indicates you have a strong interest in your child's experience and performance at school. Your efforts as a parent are a critical element in your child's education. Of course, you can't control everything, such as whether your child takes an interest in a certain subject. But you can do a great deal to support the instruction that takes place at school, enhance it in your home environment, and instill the value of education in your child.

As a parent, it's essential that you remain engaged in every step of your child's education, from the instruction that takes place in the classroom, to homework, to maintaining open lines of communication with the school. Many children get their priorities from significant adults in their lives, especially parents. To make sure that education is a priority for your child, you must take the lead.

In this chapter, I provide you with some ways to structure your home that enhance educational opportunities. I explain how to serve as a model for learning and how to provide educational resources that stimulate young minds and feed their natural curiosity. And I offer a few suggestions for what you can do to support the school's efforts at home (which I discuss in further detail in Chapter 4).

# Creating a Setting Conducive to Learning

Your home environment significantly impacts your child's education. The more ways you can create a setting that supports learning and encourages your child to value the education he receives at school, the better his chances of success. Here are a few suggestions to strengthen the educational atmosphere in your home environment:

✔ **Establish a consistent schedule and healthy routines.** Help your child establish a daily after-school routine. Allowing for time to unwind and play is certainly acceptable and something to be encouraged. However, set aside a time when your child is expected to sit down and really dig into his homework.

If your child doesn't have homework every day, have him use this time to read or engage in other educational activities. The nature of a routine is that it's consistent.

✔ **Eliminate or at least limit distractions during study/ homework time.** Designate an area in your home that's quiet and free from major distractions as the place to complete schoolwork. Your child can accomplish more and do higher-quality work with fewer distractions to lure her attention away from her studies. Major distractors include TV, video games, phones, loud music, and anything else that dilutes the mind's focus.

As your child matures, she may become aware of environmental elements that enhance her focus and productivity, such as music, so engage in conversation periodically to determine what, if anything, helps her study.

✔ **Provide access to essential materials and resources.** Give your child easy access to pencils, pens, paper, markers, a calculator, a computer with Internet access (if possible), and anything else he may need to complete his assignments. Your child shouldn't have to stop doing homework to search for materials and resources.

Carefully monitor Internet usage. The Internet is certainly a useful tool for research, but it can also become a major distraction. If your child abuses the privilege of having this resource, remove it from the study area. It's not an essential tool for meeting Common Core Standards.

✔ **Be available to answer questions and assist with homework.** Encourage your child to make an attempt to complete her homework independently. Make yourself available, but don't insist on being involved in every assignment. When she has completed her homework to the best of her ability, give the assignment a quick look to help your child correct careless errors and to be sure there are no major misunderstandings. If you notice big gaps in understanding, encourage your child to speak to her teacher the following day if possible. Trying to re-teach an entire lesson in the evenings can be hard on your child (and you)!

✔ **Attend to creature comforts.** Studies show that people are more productive in a comfortable work environment, especially if they're able to personalize their area. That's why many people display pictures and other knick-knacks in their workspaces. Encourage your child to create a workspace that's comfortable and inviting. This helps him feel at ease and takes away some of the bad stigma associated with homework.

# How to handle homework (or lack thereof)

The philosophies on assigning homework vary from teacher to teacher and school to school. Some educators assign homework as a means of getting students to practice skills and concepts at home, while others prefer to have students complete this work at school. If your child's teacher assigns homework, support the teacher's decision and help your child understand that even adults have work they must take home from time to time. If your child's teacher doesn't assign homework, you should still set aside a time and place and establish a routine for extracurricular learning, including reading, solving puzzles, exploring topics of interest, and doing hobbies. Stay in touch with the teacher and practice skills at home in fun and creative ways.

✔ **Make sure your child gets enough sleep.** A good night's sleep is one of the most important ingredients in success at school. The amount of sleep needed in order to feel energized for the next day varies with age and the individual. Generally speaking, preschoolers require 10 to 12 hours of sleep per day, which may include a nap. At 7 to 12 years old, children need 10 to 11 hours of sleep per day, and young adults (18 years and older) require 8 to 9 hours of sleep per day. Try to tune in to the optimum amount of sleep your child needs and do what you can to make sure she gets it. Being well rested is an essential part of preparation for important activities.

# Modeling Lifelong Learning

Children look to their parents and other significant adults in their lives to determine what's important to them. Because these values are instilled at an early age, it's important that you and other adults in the household communicate the importance of education and the process of learning. This includes supporting the notion that education doesn't stop when school is finished and that even adults are learners, whether or not they're still in school.

Being a lifelong learner simply means that you value education, recognize its potential, and continually seek out ways to engage in learning through various means. Even if you didn't like school as a child and young adult, being a lifelong learner can be fun because you get to decide what, when, where, and how you learn! Here are a few suggestions on how to become a lifelong learner:

✔ **Identify and study a topic that interests you.** Choose an academic subject, such as literature or a foreign language, or more practical topics, such as growing vegetables, fixing your car, or making jewelry. Part of the negativity surrounding homework is that it encroaches on time at home. You can turn the tide on feelings of resentment while bonding with your child by spending time together in study. This is a great time for your child to see you reading, researching a certain topic, or even taking a free online class.

✔ **Be the "lead reader" in your household on a daily basis.**
Make reading a regular activity in your home. Even when
homework time is over, it's a great idea to sit down and
read to or with your child, depending on her age. Find a
collection of reading materials (books, magazines, articles,
and so on) that are of interest to both of you and set aside
reading time in your daily schedule. Make reading a habit.

✔ **Point out learning opportunities in everyday life.** Be
on the lookout for ways to incorporate the skills and
concepts your child is learning into your everyday activities at home. This requires that you stay current on the
topics he's studying. (In Chapters 5 through 9, I share
summaries of the Common Core Standards for mathematics, English language arts, and literacy, along with examples of how you can reinforce the standards at home.)

✔ **Make some family time learning time.** Support your child's
interest in education by showing her how much you value
what she's studying. Ask her questions about what she
learned at school. Encourage her to respond with specifics
and give examples. This communicates to your child that
you're invested in her education and value her ability to
communicate about what she's doing at school.

✔ **Attend a class or workshop together.** Take advantage of
the educational opportunities in your community, such
as workshops offered at local stores and community centers and tours available at local, state, or national parks
and cultural centers. These are fun ways to explore new
subjects and show your child that not all learning has to
take place in a desk at school.

# Encouraging and Nurturing a Curious Mind

A significant aspect of the shift to the Common Core
Standards involves developing deep and critical thinkers who
are capable of examining information and drawing conclusions. Deep, critical thinkers are:

✔ **Honest:** When they don't know something, they admit it.
The only dumb question is the one that you don't ask!

✔ **Curious:** They're drawn to find out more about everything, especially in areas that interest them.

✔ **Eager:** Their thirst for knowledge, understanding, and skills energizes them to pursue educational opportunities and take on new challenges.

✔ **Open-minded:** They listen and are willing to entertain ideas that they may not initially agree with.

✔ **Rational:** To counter their open-mindedness, they approach what they read, see, and hear objectively and skeptically, questioning its truth and accuracy and comparing it with what they already know or think they know.

✔ **Persistent:** They don't give up until they have the information, answer, solution, or understanding they sought or at least understand the limitations of knowing (for example, the limitations in technology for unlocking the mystery of the human brain).

Some children seem to possess these qualities innately, but you can encourage your child to ask questions, seek out details, and explore the many mysteries of the world. Here are a few suggestions on how to nurture curiosity and critical thinking:

✔ **Ask "why?" and "how?"** Build a dependency on critical thinking by consistently asking your child to explain "why" and "how" answers are correct on their homework or to further develop their thoughts in casual conversations. These are good traits to build early.

✔ **Embrace the research process.** Support good research habits early and often. Whether your child is completing a homework assignment or simply asking questions about a particular subject, let him dig into some resources in print or online in order to answer his own questions. Help him get into the habit of developing a question that needs to be answered and then utilizing resources to answer that question.

✔ **Subscribe to an interesting magazine.** Validate your child's interest in a particular subject by subscribing to a magazine of her choice. If that's not a possibility, then periodically visit your local library and read magazine articles of interest.

✔ **Look behind the scenes.** Explore opportunities all around you to encourage curiosity in your child. This may involve looking at how an appliance works (your toaster, for example) or exploring a common process (such as dough rising).

✔ **Keep a record of experiences.** Encourage your child to write down information, thoughts, and other details relating to significant experiences he has when on vacations, trips, tours, or even when he sees something noteworthy on TV. This instills an appreciation for details and record-keeping. Before you know it, he'll probably be looking for new experiences to write about!

✔ **Create a space for exploration.** Designate a certain space in your home that can serve as a place to read, write, draw, color, paint, and participate in other activities that fuel your child's curiosity. If a dedicated space isn't possible, a container with materials for these activities can be put together and pulled out when the mood strikes. Add a place where you and your child can write questions that arise as you read and experience new things — for example, on a whiteboard. This is a common practice in many schools and is a good idea to replicate at home.

# Making Learning Resources Readily Available

Your child has plenty of learning resources at school — teachers, books, videos, computers with Internet access, fellow students, extracurricular activities, and so on. To truly reinforce learning at home, you need to provide additional resources, which may differ from what your child can access at school.

Team up with your child to identify and gather the resources he needs to achieve his full potential. Here's a list of suggestions to get you started:

✔ **Accumulate a collection of high-interest reading materials.** Turn reading into a fun activity at home by providing your child access to an abundance of interesting texts. Reading comprehension is strengthened over time as students consistently read more and more fluently. If you expect them to do this at home, make sure reading materials are available that are related to their interests.

✔ **Tap into resources at local museums, parks, and cultural centers.** Take advantage of any resources available around you that are readily accessible. If museums, parks, or cultural centers are nearby, visit them with your child and spend an afternoon learning together. Many places have brochures or pamphlets that summarize and highlight key features or exhibits.

✔ **Spend time at the library.** Visit your local library and explore the various resources that are available. Even though students can access numerous materials on the Internet, help your child learn to navigate the library to find reading materials. If you can't find something on your own, ask the librarian for assistance. Seeking help not only results in finding what you're looking for, but it also demonstrates the importance and value of people resources, such as librarians.

✔ **Create a file for interesting articles.** Keep track of articles in magazines and newspapers that you think will pique the interest of your child. You can simply cut them out (or print them out) and stick them in a folder. With an abundance of articles close by, you can frequently read one with your child and have a great discussion. Even if a certain article may be over her head right now, you can pull it back out in a few years.

✔ **Bookmark useful and interesting sites on the Internet.** Practice organizational skills when exploring resources on the Internet. Performing a quick search for a resource you access often is easy, but using bookmarks and favorites to flag commonly used resources facilitates and expedites the research process. Spend some time identifying certain websites that are updated frequently with materials that are interesting to your child, showing him how to bookmark or favorite the site and then prompting him to revisit the site often to read new materials.

Remain vigilant about interests and abilities outside the confines of what your child's school offers, and nurture them to the best of your ability. Enrolling your child in piano or guitar lessons or in modern-dance classes is certainly an option, but you can also explore opportunities in your community, such as community theater, church choir, local hobby clubs, and scouting. Older children may have even more opportunities, such as moot court programs in which students argue imaginary court cases in front of a mock judge or jury and even compete against other teams.

## Focus on high-interest reading materials

It's easy to get caught up in thinking that students always need to read materials that are related to what they're studying at school. However, students should also read an abundance of high-interest reading materials in order to:

- ✔ Appreciate reading as a pleasurable activity and as a form of entertainment that's often more satisfying than a TV show, video game, or movie

- ✔ Realize that reading is a way to satisfy their innate curiosity

- ✔ Establish reading fluency and improve their ability to comprehend what they've read

You don't want your child to think of reading as drudgery or as something exclusive to school studies and assignments, so make sure he's spending time on a regular basis reading what *he* wants to read.

# Making Education Relevant to the Real World

If you spend much time around school-age children, it won't take long before you hear one ask, "Why am I learning this?" If you think about it, you can't really blame him for asking. Spending time practicing abstract skills and concepts for the sake of learning isn't tempting for many children. However, it's much easier to engage in a conversation or try out a new skill when you can see the connection to everyday life. Although helping your child see the relevance of what he's studying at school requires time and effort, the outcome (an engaged and interested student) is definitely worth the investment.

You can help your child recognize the relevance of schoolwork to the real world by following these tips:

 ✔ **Help your child answer the "Why am I learning this?" question.** Don't be afraid to tackle this question with your child. Sometimes you can take a general look at the concept being studied, while other times you may have to consider using a very specific example. Either way, answering this question requires you to remain involved and aware of what your child is learning at school.

✔ **Connect skills and concepts to real-life scenarios.** Help your child connect the dots between skills and concepts taught at school and applications in real life. You can reinforce many of the math standards, particularly in the early grades, with objects around your house. You can reinforce the English language arts and literacy standards with reading materials that are interesting to your child. In Chapters 5 to 9, I provide activities that can help your child apply math, English, and other concepts and skills to the real world.

✔ **Point out the problem-solving power of knowledge.** Look for stories in the news about people solving real-world problems with knowledge and skills they probably gained in school. Your child will no doubt discover writers she likes to read, fascinating scientific discoveries, and technologies she uses on a daily basis. Help your child realize that the foundation for many human accomplishments is education.

✔ **Look ahead to potential careers.** One of the best ways to make your child's education relevant to him is to help him see how it's likely to benefit him in the future. Have a conversation with your child about a career he may be interested in pursuing. Then look for ways to connect his schoolwork to the knowledge and skills required to be successful in that career.

Research articles about how education affects brain development and discuss them with your child. You may be surprised to discover just how malleable the brain really is.

# Supporting the School's Efforts

One of the most important steps you can take in support of your child's education is to be an active participant in his school's initiatives and efforts. Getting involved not only makes you better informed about the school's expectations of your child, but it also validates the importance of school for your child. You can support your school's efforts and initiatives by doing the following:

✔ **Maintain open dialogue with your child's teacher(s).** Take advantage of every opportunity to communicate with your child's teacher(s). At the beginning of each semester, reach out to the teacher(s) and introduce yourself. Share any information that you think would be useful for them to know about your child and her progress in school. Be sure to take advantage of opportunities to participate in school events, such as open-house nights and parent-teacher conferences. Making use of e-mail to communicate on a regular basis is a great way to establish and maintain an effective relationship with your child's teacher(s).

✔ **Communicate expectations about school to your child in the same lingo the teacher uses.** Become familiar with the behavioral expectations in each of your child's classes and adopt many of the same expectations at home, using the same terminology to describe them. Teachers sometimes use this approach to maintain a consistent set of expectations from class to class. Using the same strategy at home further reinforces the school's efforts.

✔ **Brush up on grade-specific standards.** Prepare for the transition to new grades/courses by reviewing the standards for specific skills and concepts that are essential for those grade levels. Before the school year starts, practice skills and concepts from the previous grade level to make sure your child hasn't regressed during his time away from school. Then move forward with the material that's central to his upcoming grade/courses.

✔ **Know what your child is learning in each class.** Keep abreast of the topics being covered in your child's classes. A great way to do this is to review assignments and other materials that are sent home. Staying familiar with the content your child is learning allows you to support her understanding through extra practice at home. Even having basic conversations about what she learned at school on any given day communicates to your child that you value her education and are there to support her.

✔ **Keep track of your child's progress.** Don't wait until report cards come home to check on your child's progress. Review graded assignments that are sent home. Ask your child's teachers whether and how you can find out about any missing assignments or areas in which your child is struggling. Find out about any technology available that enables you to monitor your child's performance and progress and maintain contact with teachers, and then make use of these tools.

As you track your child's performance and progress, consult the Common Core Standards to determine whether your child is learning what he needs to know to achieve the standards for his current grade level.

✔ **Communicate the importance of organization and meeting deadlines.** Help your child organize her school materials in a way that's efficient and understandable to her. This may include the use of folders, binders, or other organizational methods that are reasonable for use at home and school. Teachers sometimes require their materials to be organized in a specific way, so check with your child's teacher(s) before getting started. Also consider posting a calendar in your child's work area at home that contains important dates for school. You can model this practice by doing the same by posting dates for important family events in your home. Learning to track deadlines is an important skill for students to master early.

## More resources for parents

If you're looking for even more resources to help you stay up to date with your child's education, check out the website for your state department of education for resources specific to your state. Another organization to consult is the National Parent Teacher Association at `www.pta.org`. The resources for parents on this website include grade-by-grade breakdowns of important skills and concepts, along with more ideas for parent-teacher engagement.

# Chapter 4

# Teaming Up with Teachers

**D**eveloping a positive relationship with your child's teachers and administrators is one of the most important things you can do to support your child's education. Being proactive in your efforts — not waiting for the perfect time to get involved — helps get this relationship off to a good start.

In this chapter, I give you some suggestions about how to develop and sustain a positive and helpful relationship with your child's teachers and administrators. Whether you want to improve your ability to communicate effectively and efficiently with your child's teacher, get better at helping with your child's homework, or get involved at the school, I share some things you can do to get started right away. Although it takes some effort on your part to maintain momentum after you begin, ongoing and effective parent-teacher relationships benefit everyone involved.

## Communicating Effectively with Teachers and Administrators

Your child spends a significant percentage of his time with his teachers at school. If the purpose of school was merely supervision and child-care, that would be reason enough for you to communicate consistently with teachers and administrators. But school is about much more than basic supervision. Your child is there to learn important skills, both intellectually and socially.

The progress your child makes at school will play a vital role in his success for the rest of his life. As a parent, you want to work closely with his teachers to ensure that you're supporting each other in your mutual goals for your child. It's important to communicate with your child's teachers and administrators early and often. Here's how:

✓ **Schedule a face-to-face meeting at the beginning of the year.** Reach out to your child's teachers at the start of each year and set up a time to sit down and discuss your expectations for your child's progress. This is a great time to fill the teachers in on any specific information that may be beneficial to them, such as areas in which your child often excels or tends to struggle. It's also a great time to listen to any suggestions the teachers may have for how to best support your child in the coming year.

✓ **Attend parent-teacher conferences, open houses, and other community nights at school.** Take advantage of every opportunity that the school presents to open its doors to parents, family, and community members. Involvement from key stakeholders, such as parents, is a major factor in promoting a positive and effective school culture.

✓ **Use e-mail to communicate efficiently.** Don't hesitate to send your child's teachers an e-mail when you have a question about your child's progress in class. Even if you don't have a specific concern, it's still a good idea to check in with them every week or two just to see how things are going.

✓ **Write thank-you notes.** Sending a periodic thank-you note to your child's teachers is a great way to say thanks for everything they are doing to further your child's education. Whether you write in response to a specific instance in which the teacher went out of his or her way or simply write a general "thank you," this is a tangible way of communicating that you appreciate your child's teachers and want to continue your partnership.

## Understanding how your child's school is implementing Common Core

The many schools, districts, and states that are adopting Common Core Standards are following a variety of paths to implement the standards for classroom use. You can do your part by reading up on the standards and supporting your child's efforts at home. But you can also take your understanding of the new standards a step further by finding out how your child's school is implementing the new standards.

This will let you know whether you should expect a full dose of Common Core during the current school year or whether the school is taking a gradual approach over the course of a few years. You should also take this opportunity to obtain a copy of the standards that your child's school is using, because states can add up to 15 percent more content to the Common Core Standards.

✔ **Take a trip to the principal's office.** Schedule a time to stop by the school one day, or during a specific school event, to introduce yourself to the school's administrators. Take this opportunity to find out more about the school. Ask whether the school has programs that may be beneficial for your child and how you can be involved in supporting the mission of the school.

# Monitoring Your Child's Performance and Progress

To make sure that your child is showing adequate progress at school, it's essential that you keep track of how he is doing when it comes to mastery of important skills and concepts.

The process that each teacher and school follows for communicating about student progress varies. Schools may send home reports at designated intervals or provide access to an online grade portal. Regardless of the methods used by your child's school, you can find many ways to monitor your child's performance at school.

> ✔ **Examine results on graded assignments, quizzes, and tests.** Check with your child frequently about graded assignments that are sent home. Some teachers send graded work home on specific days, while others send it home as they grade it. At the beginning of the year, find out how your child's teacher communicates grades and then be consistent in monitoring your child's progress.

REMEMBER

Some schools use standards-based grading, which means that you may not see letter grades (A, B, C, and so on) on every assignment. Standards-based grading involves communicating student progress on individual skills and concepts. For example, instead of having an A+ in Grade 3 math, your child may receive a report that indicates mastery of addition and subtraction, partial mastery of multiplication and division, and so on. The terminology used in standards-based grading varies from school to school, but the emphasis is on providing specific, actionable information on individual learning standards.

> ✔ **Gauge how efficiently your child completes assignments.** Don't wait on grades to find out how your child is progressing. Educators use something called *formative assessment* to monitor student progress. This involves assessing how accurately and efficiently students can complete tasks that don't necessarily have grades attached to them. You can do the same thing at home by keeping track of how successfully your child completes his homework, identifying whether he struggles or completes it with ease. Keeping up with grades and teacher feedback on assignments that are sent home from school is an easy way to see how your child is doing.

> ✔ **Communicate frequently with the teachers to check on your child's progress on important standards.** Reach out on a regular basis to discuss your child's progress on skills and concepts that are essential to his grade or course. How often you need to check in on your child's progress depends on how well he is doing at school. If he is successfully mastering new skills and concepts, you may not need to check in with the teacher as often. If your child struggles, however, you may want to check in with the teacher every few days or on a weekly basis to make sure you can support him at home.

In Chapters 5–9, I review many of the components of the Common Core Standards in math, English language arts, and literacy. Based on your review of the standards and the expectations outlined by your child's teachers, keep tabs on how well your child is moving along.

Identify important skills and concepts at the beginning of the year. Your child's teachers should be able to send you a list of these items.

✔ **Speak openly with your child regarding his understanding of skills and concepts.** Make time to discuss important content on a regular basis. This can be as simple as asking him a few quick questions about what he learned at school or the nature of any homework he may have. Be sure to discuss specifics so you have a chance to probe his understanding of the skills and concepts contained in his schoolwork.

✔ **Celebrate success when he catches on to a skill or concept quickly.** Don't forget to be your child's cheerleader when he has success with a particular skill or concept. It's easy to get overly focused on the areas where he struggles because you're trying to be supportive and help him along. However, it's important to remember that he needs to hear from you when he's doing well, too.

Be specific when you give positive feedback to your child. If he does something well, tell him *exactly* what he did correctly. This helps to reinforce particular habits and ways of thinking, increasing the likelihood that he will repeat these actions in the future.

✔ **Don't back away from challenging content.** Be persistent if your child is learning content that he (or even you) finds particularly difficult. If he is struggling with a particular concept, take advantage of the resources that are available to you. If it's a specific Common Core Standard, consult the summaries and examples in Chapters 5–9.

You can also find many online resources that break down the Common Core Standards. If you or your child is struggling with another aspect of the material he is learning, reach out to your child's teachers for help.

# Handling homework frustrations

Expect for homework to induce some frustrations from time to time. The directions can seem so clear to your child when he is sitting and listening to his teachers at school, but sometimes things can get a bit fuzzy by the time he gets home. To reduce frustrations, try these tips:

✔ Give your child an agenda or planner to record homework assignments.

✔ Remind your child to write down the directions instead of trying to remember them word for word.

✔ Keep important tools and resources (such as paper, pens, pencils, calculators, tape, and so on) in a consistent location.

✔ Step away from homework if it gets overly confusing and try again after taking a break — it may even be necessary on rare occasions to write a note and allow the teacher to help the next day.

✔ Avoid trying to complete homework during other events that are going on in the house (such as family gatherings, meals, and so on).

Following these simple tips can eliminate some of the stressors associated with completing homework. After all, you want your child's full attention to be on the content and not on outside distractions.

# Helping with Homework

Another important role you can play in support of your child's learning is to ensure that he has a proper environment in which to complete assignments at home. Teachers have differing philosophies and policies on the nature and frequency of homework, but you can take a number of actions to assist your child regardless of how much homework he has on a regular basis.

✔ **Have a time and place for homework.** Set a specific routine for accomplishing homework when your child gets home from school. It's certainly acceptable to take a break and unwind after a tough day at school, but you want to make sure he tackles his homework before it gets too late in the evening. If no homework is assigned, take the opportunity to simply have a conversation with your child about what he learned at school that day.

✔ **Don't micromanage during homework.** Don't stand over your child's shoulder while he's doing homework. Make sure your child understands the directions for his assignment, stand back, and let him dig in. If you lend a helping hand too quickly, your child soon learns that you'll do the work for him at the first sign of difficulty. Let your child have an opportunity to ask for help before you offer your assistance. Teachers refer to this as "wait time."

✔ **Read up on essential skills and concepts.** Look ahead to important content that your child will encounter and read up on the unfamiliar material (which will vary depending on your comfort level with certain concepts).

✔ **Ask questions when homework gets tricky.** Reach out to the teacher if the going gets tough. If your child has difficulty with particular skills or concepts, his teachers will most certainly want to know so they can supplement his learning in some way. Apart from directly contacting the teacher, check to see whether the teacher has a school-based website or other resources that can help you out.

✔ **Check for a homework policy.** If you aren't seeing homework on a regular basis, make sure the school doesn't have a policy that outlines how much and how often homework is sent home. Some schools think that less is more, while others include homework on a regular basis.

# Volunteering at School

It's easy to overlook the importance of volunteering your time, but lending a hand at school events is a great way to stay engaged. Not only do you build relationships with teachers, staff members, and other parents, but you also show your child that you value the school and the service it provides to your family.

Most schools offer a variety of ways for parents to get involved, but here are a few ideas to get you started:

✔ **Join the parent-teacher association (PTA).** Get involved with the PTA (it may be called something different) at your child's school. These organizations are often key channels of information within the school and provide a great way for you to connect with teachers and other parents.

✔ **Take the lead on a fundraiser.** Contact your child's teacher to find out whether you can help organize an upcoming fundraiser. Schools are constantly raising money to buy new books, technology, and other resources. This is a great way to improve the resources available in your child's class or school.

✔ **Lend your skills for special projects.** Don't be afraid to offer up any skills or experience you may have. Schools often need assistance with building projects, artwork, graphic design, and other projects that require special skill sets. If you think you can help out, contact your child's school.

Before you can get involved in school activities that involve other children, you will probably have to complete a background check, drug test, and other paperwork required by the school. Be sure to plan ahead and take care of these requirements ahead of time so you aren't delayed in helping with your child's team or organization.

✔ **Offer to help with test administration.** Reach out to see whether your help is needed during the administration of standardized tests. Schools often need help counting test materials, pencils, rulers, calculators, and other items used during testing. Parents and community members are also sometimes needed as proctors to help teachers monitor the classrooms.

✔ **Organize a donation drive for books or materials.** Be proactive in addressing needs that arise at your child's school. This may include sponsoring a drive to collect books, school supplies, or other materials the teachers need. Most schools have policies on taking donations from parents and community members, so check with your child's teachers or administrators before collecting anything you intend to donate.

# Part II

# Acquainting Yourself with the Standards

## *Five Simple Ways to Track Your Child's Progress on the Standards*

Organize a folder for each subject and keep any graded assignments that are sent home from school.

Print a copy of the standards for your child's grade level and write notes about her success on certain skills and content, along with areas where she is more challenged.

Encourage your child to reflect on her own learning in a journal or another record-keeping medium. This enables you and your child to keep track of what she is learning in her own words.

Color code standards based on how easy or difficult they are for your child. Choose colors for easy, somewhat challenging, and difficult standards and use highlighters to mark through them. This allows you to quickly refer to areas of difficulty.

Create a consistent schedule for communicating with your child's teacher in person, on the phone, or via e-mail.

For tips on tackling concerns about your child's school-work, check out the free article at www.dummies.com/extras/commoncoreforparents.

# In this part. . .

✔ Find out about the math skills and concepts addressed in kindergarten through Grade 8.

✔ Take a look at the math standards in Grades 9-12.

✔ Review the expectations of the English language arts standards in kindergarten through Grade 5.

✔ Read about the English language arts standards in Grades 6-12.

✔ See how the literacy standards are incorporated into history/ social studies, science, and technical subjects in Grades 6-12.

# Chapter 5

# Doing the Math in Kindergarten through Grade 8

*C*ommon Core math standards for kindergarten through Grade 8 focus on essential math concepts and skills that students are likely to need for their entire lives, especially as they try to grasp higher-level math in high school and beyond. In Chapter 2, I describe the Common Core math standards in general terms so you can wrap your brain around them as a whole. This chapter gets down to the nitty-gritty, explaining what elementary and junior high school students need to know after completing each grade level and how you can help them succeed.

## Looking at K–8 Content Standards

The Common Core content standards for math cover a variety of domains (for example, algebraic thinking, fractions, and geometry) that repeat from grade to grade, as shown in Figure 5-1. (See Chapter 2 for more about domains.) However, the specific skills required in each grade change from grade to grade, building on knowledge and skills taught in prior grades. This structure allows for a considerable amount of coherence as the major domains flow and build from one grade to the next. Because specific skills are rarely repeated, however, mastery at the appropriate grade level is very important to ensure success in the next grade.

| Math Standards | Grades | | | | | | | | |
|---|---|---|---|---|---|---|---|---|---|
| | K | 1 | 2 | 3 | 4 | 5 | 6 | 7 | 8 |
| Counting & Cardinality | √ | | | | | | | | |
| Operations & Algebraic Thinking | √ | √ | √ | √ | √ | √ | | | |
| Numbers & Operations in Base Ten | √ | √ | √ | √ | √ | √ | | | |
| Measurement & Data | √ | √ | √ | √ | √ | √ | | | |
| Geometry | √ | √ | √ | √ | √ | √ | √ | √ | √ |
| Number & Operations: Fractions | | | | √ | √ | √ | √ | | |
| Ratios & Proportional Relationships | | | | | | | √ | √ | |
| The Number System | | | | | | | √ | √ | √ |
| Expressions & Equations | | | | | | | √ | √ | √ |
| Statistics and Probability | | | | | | | √ | √ | √ |
| Functions | | | | | | | | | √ |

**Figure 5-1:** Common Core Mathematics Standards K–8

In the following sections, I introduce and summarize the skills and concepts students are expected to master by the end of each grade level and offer suggestions on how you, as a parent, can help your child meet those expectations. (I recommend that you read detailed descriptions of the Common Core Standards for each grade level at www.corestandards.org.)

# Meeting Numbers and Shapes in Kindergarten

In kindergarten, math focuses on two areas:

- ✓ **Whole numbers:** Whole numbers are those that aren't fractions; for example, 1 and 99 are whole numbers, whereas ⅓ is not. Kindergarten students are expected to be able to count, use written numerals to represent numbers, and combine and remove objects to grasp the concepts of addition and subtraction without necessarily solving written equations, such as $2 + 2 = 4$. For example, a student should be able to tell you that if you have five apples, and Janice eats one, only four apples remain.

✔ **Shapes:** By the end of kindergarten, students should be familiar with two-dimensional shapes (circles, squares, triangles, and so on), three-dimensional shapes (cubes, cylinders, and cones, for example), orientation (the position of a shape in the space it occupies), and spatial relationships (the position of shapes in relation to other shapes). Students are also expected to know the vocabulary or how to talk about shapes and related concepts.

Kindergarten math standards focus on only two areas (numbers and shapes), but the essential concepts and skills are divided into five different domains.

# Counting and cardinality

In kindergarten, the focus is on counting with *cardinal numbers* (1, 2, 3, and so on) and *ordinal numbers* (1st, 2nd, 3rd, and so on). Students discover what numbers are and what they represent, how to write numerals from 0 to 20, and how to count from 1 to 100 by ones and tens. Students also use numbers to count objects in a group and discover how to count higher to add an item to the group. Understanding the relationships between the numeral and how a number represents a certain quantity also enables them to compare the number of items in different groups, whether they are working with manipulative objects or numbers on a page.

Write the number 5 on a piece of paper. Ask your child to tell what the number means or represents. Provide objects to count out, such as blocks or dice, to show you how many 5 represents. Practice counting from 1 to 100, sometimes adding a degree of difficulty by alternating the number used to start the series. Encourage your child to count everyday objects in your home that can be put in certain groups (such as pillows, utensils, or apples), while placing emphasis on the final number in the set he counts.

# Operations and algebraic thinking

At the kindergarten level, the operations and algebraic thinking domain applies mostly to addition and subtraction. Students are expected to understand the concept of *decomposing numbers* — showing that a number, such as 9, can be separated into parts, such as 4 and 5. This is more than just learning basic addition facts, as students demonstrate their understanding of the numbers that can combine to make a larger number. Students also practice adding and subtracting with objects, fingers, verbal explanations, drawings, acting out situations (for example, adding fellow students to an existing group), and so on.

Use ordinary objects, such as forks or spoons, to practice addition and subtraction. Mix it up by creating a game-like atmosphere and see how quickly your child can complete basic addition and subtraction using numbers from 1 to 5. Use ordinary objects to demonstrate the concept of decomposing a number; for example, divide a group of five marbles into two groups, one with three and the other with two marbles.

## Number and operations in base ten

In kindergarten, *base ten* refers to the value of a number from 1 to 9 according to its position in a number greater than 9; for example, in the number 15, the value of 1 is actually 10. Students practice using place value with numbers from 11 to 19 by describing that the number in the tens place (the left digit) is made up of ten ones, and the number in the ones place (the right digit) is counted by ones.

Reinforce your child's understanding of place value by writing a number from 11 to 19 on a piece of paper and then having your child draw or write the total number or quantity represented by the left and right numerals. Have your child double check his answer by counting all of the objects he draws or writes. To raise the bar, have your child decompose numbers from 11 to 19 using one group of 10 and another group for the rest. To further reinforce the concept of base ten, show your child a group of more than ten objects and ask him to identify how many groups of 10 can be made. Then allow him to count the group(s) of ten, separating each object from the original group as he counts.

# Measurement and data

At the kindergarten level, the measurement and data domain concentrates on two concepts and skills:

- ✔ An object's comparable attributes, such as length, height, and weight.

- ✔ Measuring and comparing measurable attributes in two objects, such as the lengths of two crayons.

Students are expected to compare objects for different purposes and to describe their results. They also use their understanding of measurements to compare, contrast, or classify multiple objects based on how their attributes (such as length, height, and so on) are related.

Have your child compare the attributes of different objects and rank them based on their length, height, width, weight, and so on. Even though comparing and contrasting these characteristics is a major emphasis in kindergarten, you can extend his understanding of measurements by introducing him to basic tools, such as a ruler, and allowing him to practice taking accurate measurements.

# Geometry

Kindergarten students are expected to describe shapes and where objects are located in relation to other objects, along with composing simple shapes to form larger shapes. Students use these concepts to build a sense of familiarity with the names of objects, determine whether the objects exist in two or three dimensions, and recognize certain shapes in real-world settings.

Help your child become familiar with the shapes of commonly used objects and where they can be found in everyday life; for example, an orange is round (as described in two dimensions) or a sphere (in three dimensions). Assist her in recognizing objects in the home environment that are the same as geometric shapes or that can be put together to make different shapes; for example, use paper, books, glasses or cups, and boxes to reinforce her ability to recognize shapes in two and three dimensions.

# Stepping Up with Numbers, Operations, and Shapes in Grade 1

In Grade 1, students expand their skills with numbers and incorporate the use of more numbers and details when solving math problems and looking at shapes. Common Core Standards for Grade 1 emphasize four areas:

✔ **Addition and subtraction of whole numbers:** Students develop a more sophisticated understanding of addition and subtraction as they grasp the concepts of add to, take from, put together, and take apart. They may also use comparison subtraction, in which they determine how many more objects are in one group than another. They also acquire strategies for solving addition and subtraction problems more quickly and easily.

✔ **Whole number relationships and place value:** Working primarily with numbers from 1 to 100, students begin to recognize numbers in terms of tens and ones, and use this understanding to solve addition and subtraction problems more easily.

✔ **Length measurements:** Students develop an understanding of how to measure in units and how to indirectly compare the measurement of two objects by comparing each object to a third object; for example, if Jill is taller than Joe and Jen is shorter than Joe, Jill is taller than Jen. However, the third object used to compare the heights of Jill and Joe may also be a nonstandard unit of measure, such as a paper clip. Practicing comparing the measurements of multiple objects (especially when the objects aren't similar) helps your child transfer his understanding of measurements to a wider range of objects that he'll see in everyday life.

✔ **Composing and decomposing two- and three-dimensional shapes:** Students combine and separate two- and three-dimensional shapes and compare shapes in preparation for understanding properties such as congruence and symmetry.

In the following sections, I explain how these four areas are addressed in the four domains that are the focus in Grade 1.

# Operations and algebraic thinking

Addition and subtraction using the numbers 1 to 20 are the primary focus. Students use counting to add on or take away numbers in addition and subtraction problems and practice determining whether equations are true or false.

With a set of concrete objects, give your child groups of objects (such as five spoons and four forks) to add together. In this example, she would count up to nine utensils. Then ask her to write the equation for the problem she just solved — for example, $5 + 4 = 9$.

# Number and operations in base ten

Students count to 120 and dig deeper into the concept of place value. Students demonstrate that any number in the tens place represents a certain number of tens. For example, 30 is 3 sets of 10, 80 is 8 sets of 10, and so on. The symbols > (greater than), < (less than), and = (equal to) are used to compare two-digit numbers, and students begin to add and subtract with one- and two-digit numbers within 100.

Continue practicing with place value. Compare the value of numbers using the tens place by using the symbols >, <, and = with numbers from 10 to 90. Challenge your child to explain why numbers are smaller or larger than others by referencing the value of numbers in the tens place.

# Measurement and data

The use of measuring continues, including ordering multiple objects by their length and using the length of other objects to indirectly measure and order an object. Students discover how to tell and write time using digital and analog clocks, and they begin to use basic data, such as the number of forks and spoons in your kitchen, to compare and contrast different categories.

Have your child rearrange objects in your home by length — shortest to longest or vice versa. Reinforce your child's ability to communicate the correct time of day by telling and writing time at various periods during the morning, afternoon, and evening.

## Geometry

In Grade 1, students are expected to recognize attributes of shapes and which attributes define certain shapes, such as that a rectangle has four sides, that a circle is round, and so on. Students combine shapes in two and three dimensions to create other shapes and divide shapes into parts. They also become familiar with the concepts and terms half, fourth, and quarter.

Incorporate learning into meal-times by having your child practice using the terms half, fourth, and quarter during food preparation. You can also incorporate these skills into playtime with any object that can be separated or divided.

# Laying the Groundwork for Multiplication in Grade 2

In Grade 2, students begin to build a conceptual foundation for multiplication as they think about combining groups when adding. Students continue to encounter more complex concepts; build on their previous understanding of place value; and increase the precision of measurements with time, money, and objects by using standard units of measure.

Common Core Standards in Grade 2 focus on four areas:

- ✔ **Addition and subtraction in preparation for multiplication:** An emphasis on adding and subtracting equal groups of numbers prepares students to multiply groups of objects in later grades.

- ✔ **Use of the base ten number system in addition and subtraction:** Students extend their use of base ten when adding and subtracting numbers up to 1,000.

- ✔ **Using standard units of measure:** Students use centimeters, inches, seconds, minutes, and other standard units of measure to take measurements.

- ✔ **Describing and analyzing shapes:** Students learn to use the sides and angles of shapes to compare and contrast them to other shapes. This helps them understand attributes of shapes, such as area and volume, that are used in later grades.

In the following sections, I explain how these areas of focus are applied in relation to the four domains in Grade 2.

## Operations and algebraic thinking

In Grade 2, students work toward gaining fluency in adding and subtracting numbers from 1 to 20 and solving addition and subtraction word problems with numbers from 1 to 100. Some problems may require multiple steps. Finding the total number of items by combining equal groups provides a basis for multiplication in later grades.

Help your child prepare for multiplication by working with equal groups of objects. For example, put three groups of two pieces of cereal on the table. Ask her to say how many groups there are and how many objects are in each group. Then ask her to count the total. She will see that three groups of two equal six. Recognizing the combination of equal groups is important in strengthening her conceptual foundation for understanding multiplication. If this is too difficult at first, let your child practice skip counting by twos, threes, and fives to further support her understanding of combining equal groups of numbers.

## Number and operations in base ten

Place value extends to include the hundreds place, and students practice counting by fives, tens, and hundreds. Students are also able to write numbers up to 1,000 using numerals, names of numbers, and expanded forms (for example, writing 1,727 as 1,000 + 700 + 20 + 7). Students are also expected to add and subtract in their heads using tens and hundreds.

Practice counting using fives, tens, and hundreds, backward and forward. This is a simple way to build fluency in counting and reinforce skills in addition and subtraction. Writing some of these numbers in expanded form also supports the understanding of place value. You can also ask your child questions like "How many tens are there in 215?" to see if she can identify that there are 21 tens.

## *Measurement and data*

Use of specific units, such as centimeters and inches, requires students to be precise with measurements. Students begin to apply previously acquired skills in addition and subtraction to measurements. They also practice telling time to the nearest five-minute increment, using money and related symbols to solve word problems, and using graphs to represent collected data.

Have your child measure objects around the house using different units of measurement, such as inches, feet, centimeters, and meters. Remember to make him be specific! Ask your child to measure something in sections and add the measurements. Periodically ask your child to tell you the time to the nearest five-minute increment.

## *Geometry*

The use of shapes becomes more complex, and students are expected to recognize specific characteristics of geometric shapes, such as the concept that a triangle has three sides and three angles, and a cube has six equal faces. Students continue to divide shapes into multiple equal parts, including halves, thirds, and fourths.

Ask your child to recognize different shapes, including triangles, rectangles, cubes, pentagons, and hexagons, and to describe their characteristics. Practice drawing shapes and having your child divide them into equal parts. Be sure to let her work with a variety of shapes and make her verbalize the parts into which she is dividing shapes (halves, thirds, or fourths).

# *Multiplying, Dividing, and Meeting Fractions in Grade 3*

Multiplication, division, and fractions are key components of the skills and concepts students encounter in Grade 3. Students also continue to work with shapes.

Common Core Standards in Grade 3 focus on three key areas:

- **Multiplication and division:** Students multiply and divide whole numbers with numbers from 1 to 100. They use various strategies to support their understanding of the relationship between multiplication and division.

- **Fractions:** Students begin to work with *unit fractions* — those that have 1 as the numerator, such as ½ and ⅓.

- **Two-dimensional shapes:** Students use the characteristics of two-dimensional shapes, such as sides and angles, to explain similarities and differences between shapes.

 If your child struggles with these concepts initially, refer to a previous grade level where the ways of thinking needed to understand multiplication, division, and fractions are introduced. For example, you may engage your child in adding equal groups of objects (as in Grade 2) to better understand the concept of multiplication.

## Operations and algebraic thinking

In Grade 3, students continue to practice multiplication while being introduced to the concept of division. Students multiply and divide using numbers 1 to 100, and use addition, subtraction, multiplication, and division to solve word problems with two steps. Students also work to find patterns that exist when multiplying numbers.

 Practice multiplication and division within 100 until your child can complete the calculations with minimal hesitation. Start with easier tasks, such as multiplying and dividing with small numbers and increments of five, and progress in difficulty. Look for ways to incorporate multiplication and division in everyday activities, such as calculating the number of dimes in a dollar or the number of nickels in a quarter.

## Number and operations in base ten

Students round to the nearest 10 or 100 and add or subtract numbers from 1 to 1,000 using their understanding of the ones, tens, and hundreds places. Multiplication using single digit numbers and increments of 10 (using 10 to 90) is also incorporated.

Reinforce your child's understanding of place value by encouraging him to describe the value of the ones, tens, and hundreds places in relation to each other with each practice problem that he tries. Make this relevant by using the ages of your family members to compare and contrast ages with an emphasis on place value.

## Number and operations: Fractions

Grade 3 math builds an understanding of fractions as parts of a whole. This includes identifying fractions on a number line and comparing the size or amount of fractions; for example, ½ is larger than ⅓.

The concept of a fraction can be difficult to comprehend at first, so keep it simple and relate it to real-world applications. Use everyday objects to represent a part of a whole. Start with an even group of objects, such as four spoons. Have your child verbalize that one spoon is one out of four, or ¼. Repeated practice in this manner helps to take the fear out of fractions.

Food items work great in demonstrating fractions. Cut an apple in half or a pizza in eight equal slices. Ask your child to verbalize that half an apple is one out of two or ½ and have her write the fraction. With the pizza, you can count each slice as a part of the whole. The main point is that she understand how to count fractional units and how to compare them to the number of units that make up the whole.

## Measurement and data

Measurement skills expand to include estimation and further degrees of detail. Data is presented in various forms and with multiple categories, such as a chart or graph that shows responses or results from a survey with multiple questions administered to several people. Students tell time to the nearest minute and expand their understanding of shapes by finding the perimeter of a shape and using multiplication to find the area of rectangles. They also estimate and measure liquid volumes using standard units.

Continue to focus on details, such as telling time to the minute and describing characteristics of shapes. Focus more on the parts of a shape (for example, sides, perimeter, and diameter) rather than the shape itself to reinforce your child's understanding of area and perimeter. Have your child measure the bedrooms to determine their area in square feet and determine who in the family has the largest and smallest bedrooms.

## Geometry

Students continue to use characteristics of shapes to classify them into categories. Fractions are also incorporated as students practice expressing parts of shapes as fractions related to the whole.

Take another opportunity to work with fractions as they relate to the area of shapes. Use building blocks or objects that can be stacked together as a whole. Have your child measure the total area of the rectangle constructed by the blocks. Then instruct your child to divide the shape into two equal parts and measure the area again. Talk to your child about the relationship between her first measurement of the entire area and her second measurement of the two smaller shapes.

# Gaining Expertise in Multiplication, Division, and Shapes in Grade 4

After getting a handle on the basics of multiplying, dividing, and using fractions in Grade 3, Grade 4 students put their skills to work by applying these concepts to multistep word problems, finding equivalent fractions, representing data, and measuring and classifying angles. Specifically, Common Core Standards in Grade 4 math focus on these three areas:

- ✔ **Multiplication and division:** Students move up to multiplying and dividing by multidigit numbers.

- ✔ **Fractions:** Understanding of fractions expands to include using *fractional equivalence* as the comparison of fractions with different numerators and denominators (for example, ⅜ is equal to ½), adding and subtracting fractions and mixed numbers with unlike denominators, and multiplying a fraction by a whole number.

✔ **Classifying shapes:** Students classify and compare shapes based on their characteristics, such as angles, number of sides, whether the sides are parallel or perpendicular, and so on.

In the following sections, I explain how these areas apply to the five domains in Grade 4.

## Operations and algebraic thinking

In Grade 4, students begin to use multiplication to solve multistep word problems, including using a letter to represent an unknown number. Students also progress toward understanding the concept that the order in which two numbers are multiplied doesn't matter; for example, $2 \times 3$ is equal to $3 \times 2$. Factoring numbers from 1 to 100 (for example, $100 = 5 \times 20$) and using number patterns is also incorporated into this domain.

Write out word problems for your child to complete using math skills your child has already acquired. It's important for her to be able to transfer skills from number problems to word problems without losing sight of the central math concept. Help her distinguish essential from nonessential information when solving problems.

## Number and operations in base ten

In Grade 4, students use their understanding of place value in the tens and hundreds place to divide numbers and to compare the value of multidigit numbers. Addition, subtraction, multiplication, and division with multidigit numbers continue to reinforce place value.

Continue practicing math problems with multidigit numbers in order to build familiarity and fluency. It's essential for your child to grasp place value in the tens and hundreds places, so make him explain the place value of each part of every problem.

# Number and operations: Fractions

In this domain, students extend the use of fractions to finding equivalent fractions and develop an understanding that two fractions can be equivalent even though they don't consist of the exact same numbers (for example, ⅓ is equal to ²⁄₆). They also compare fractions with different numerators (the top number) and denominators (the bottom number). Students are required to decompose fractions into simpler fractions that equal the original fraction, multiply by whole numbers, and write fractions that are already equivalent to tenths, hundredths, and thousandths as decimals.

Practice fractions at home as often as possible. Continue to use everyday objects to demonstrate fractions, including comparing equivalent fractions and fractions with different numerators and denominators. For example, if you cut a pizza into eight slices, ask your child how many slices the family would need to eat to eat ½ or ¾ of the pizza. Concrete displays of fractions reinforce that fractions are parts of the whole.

# Measurement and data

In Grade 4, students discover how to express measurements as being relative to other measurements, and they solve word problems that incorporate the measurement of various objects. They also plot data in the form of fractions on a line and can compare the sizes or amounts represented by different points on the graph. Students also begin to understand angle measurements and the tools used to measure angles.

Practice ordering fractions on a number line. Reinforce your child's understanding of sizes with fractions by using small objects or drawings to represent each fraction. Start with fractions that have the same denominator at first. After your child demonstrates mastery of comparing fractions that have the same denominator, make the exercise more difficult by introducing fractions with different denominators.

## Geometry

Students draw lines and angles and can classify the type of angle (right, acute, and obtuse). They also use a line of symmetry to fold a shape into equal parts.

Practice using a protractor to measure angles. Have your child compare the size of angles and classify the angles as right, acute, or obtuse. Make sure she explains why each measured angle is right, acute, or obtuse in order to support her understanding of the angle types. Encourage your child to recognize lines of symmetry and angles in real-world objects, such as the vertical line that separates two sides of a face or the angle of a ramp leading into a building.

# Honing Skills in Fractions, Division, and Volume in Grade 5

In Grade 5, students encounter new components in math problems, such as brackets and parentheses. Certain concepts introduced in earlier grades, such as working with fractions and decimals, are more specialized and are used in multiplication and division. Students also continue to look at representations of data and take their first steps in graphing points on a coordinate plane. Common Core Standards for Grade 5 math call for a focus on three key areas:

- ✔ **Fractions:** Students develop fluency with multiplying fractions and a conceptual understanding of the procedures used to multiply fractions.

- ✔ **Division:** Students hone their skills in division by dividing by two-digit divisors and developing an understanding of decimal fractions and the place values of numbers that come after the decimal point.

- ✔ **Volume:** Grade 5 math introduces the concept of the volume of three-dimensional objects.

## Operations and algebraic thinking

Mathematical calculations are extended in this domain. Students discover how to complete expressions that include brackets, parentheses, and other symbols in order to grasp the order of operations. The order of operations rules govern the sequence in which you perform operations (such as addition, subtraction, and multiplication) in multioperation equations. The order goes like this:

- ✔ Parentheses and exponents
- ✔ Multiplication and division
- ✔ Addition and subtraction

For example, in this equation

$$(4 \times 2) + 3^2 - (9 \div 3)^2 \times 5 =$$

you perform the operations in the following sequence:

1. Operations in parentheses first, which gives you:

   $(8) + 3^2 - (3)^2 \times 5 =$

2. Exponents, which gives you:

   $(8) + 9 - 9 \times 5 =$

3. Multiplication, which gives you:

   $(8) + 9 - 45 =$

4. Addition, which gives you:

   $17 - 45 =$

5. Subtraction, which gives you the final result:

   $-28$

In addition to order of operations, students are introduced to patterns with more than one rule, and they graph pairs of numbers from a pattern on a coordinate plane.

Practice solving problems that require multiple operations to reinforce your child's understanding of the order of operations. Help him come up with a way to remember the order of operations so that he doesn't get confused when working problems.

Don't let your child get lost in the new details. Help him understand how symbols such as brackets and parentheses are used in the order of operations so that he stays on track.

# Number and operations in base ten

Grade 5 math applies the concept of place value to decimals. Students see that each place is ⅒ of the place to the left, and students are challenged to add, subtract, multiply, and divide by numbers with decimals to the thousandths place.

Write a series of numbers that includes decimals up to the thousandths place. Ask your child to explain the value of each place in the number, including comparing the value of the place held by digits within the same number. Then give her a multidigit number, such as 23.45, and ask her to tell you how many tenths and hundredths there are. This encourages your child to develop a deeper understanding of the relationship between the places.

# Number and operations: Fractions

In Grade 5, students take another look at adding and subtracting with *mixed numbers* (a whole number with a fraction) and fractions that have different denominators, including their use in word problems. Students also discover how to multiply and divide fractions by other fractions, including in real-world situations where fractions are used.

Practice adding and subtracting mixed numbers and fractions that have different denominators. Continue using everyday objects to represent fractions. Be sure to represent the whole number in a mixed number with whole unit(s) of the objects so that your child begins to understand that the mixed number is a whole number added to a fraction.

# Measurement and data

Students begin to convert units into other units (for example, feet into inches) and are able to do so in real-world problems. Volume is added as a characteristic of solid figures, and students explore various ways to measure volume in rectangular prisms with edges represented by whole numbers.

Convert units of measure by using a ruler or other tool to measure a rectangular object, such as a large book or a box of cereal. Then have your child convert inches into feet. You can use the formulas for volume (volume = length × width × height, or volume = base × height) to find the volume of the same object. Ask your child to describe what volume represents for each object measured.

## Geometry

Students graph points on a coordinate plane and identify the location and use of the $X$ axis and $Y$ axis when graphing an ordered pair. They find out how to solve real-world problems by graphing ordered pairs in the first quadrant (when both numbers are positive). They also use characteristics of shapes to classify them into one or more categories with other similar shapes. For example, students may be asked to explain how a square can be a rectangle and a rhombus at the same time (even though a rhombus is not a rectangle).

Help your child get comfortable with the coordinate plane by practicing graphing various sets of ordered pairs. Reinforce the use of the $X$ axis and $Y$ axis by asking your child to explain why she places the points in the ordered pairs in particular locations. Look for graphs in newspapers and magazines and ask your child to explain what the graph shows.

# Exploring Ratios, Rates, Variables, Exponents, and More in Grade 6

Grade 6 math introduces students to new skills involving the use of ratios and unit rate, absolute value, and variables and exponents to extend students' abilities to use math to solve a variety of problems. Geometry expands to include the calculation of area and volume, while statistics is introduced as a means of learning about a population.

# Ratios and proportional relationships

Students encounter new concepts in this domain as they take a look at ratios and unit rate for the first time. A *ratio* is a comparison between two numbers; for example, if you have 7 dogs and 12 cats, the ratio of dogs to cats is 7 to 12 or 7:12. A unit rate is a ratio that compares a number to a singular quantity, such as miles per gallon (mpg) or dollars per pound. They describe ratios in terms of their relationship with the singular quantity to express amounts using unit rate. Students use both concepts to solve real-world problems.

Take advantage of meal preparation as a teachable moment. This is a great opportunity to show your child what ratios look like and how they are used in real-life situations. Look at the sticker on a package of meat purchased at the store (hide the price per pound) and have your child explain how much it costs per pound based on the number of pounds and the total price. For example, if a package of ground beef costs $7 and weighs four pounds, your child can divide 7 by 4 to determine how much the meat costs per pound ($1.75).

# The number system

The number system domain overlaps considerably with operations. Grade 6 students find out how to divide fractions by fractions, and use addition, subtraction, multiplication, and division to fluently solve problems with multidigit numbers. Students encounter negative numbers and describe the relationship between positive and negative numbers on a number line. They also encounter the concept of absolute value — a number's distance from zero on a number line regardless of whether the number is to the right or the left of zero. The distance from zero is always a positive measurement. This number system includes the use of *rational numbers* — whole numbers and fractions.

Reinforce absolute value with positive and negative numbers using a number line and a small object. Draw a number line starting at negative 10 on the left, zero in the middle, and positive 10 on the right with intervals of 1. Place an object on a positive or negative number and ask your child to tell how far away the object is from zero. Ask your child to describe the number in terms of absolute value, or the distance from zero. Repeat with different numbers of objects placed on positive and negative numbers. Remember that no matter how far the number is from zero on the number line, the absolute value of the number is always positive.

Avoid confusion with fractions by continually reminding your child that a fraction is only a part of a whole. This especially helps when dividing fractions. For example, if your child needs to divide 6 by 2, ask her how many groups of 2 are in 6, with the answer being 3. If your child needs to divide ¾ by ½, use the same logic. How many groups of ½ are in ¾? She'll find one whole group of ½ and half of another group of ½ in ¾.

## Expressions and equations

Students use symbols (such as $x$ and $y$) to represent and solve for unknown quantities in equations. They're also introduced to the use of exponents in equations. An *exponent* is a number that appears above and to the right of a number to indicate how many times it must be multiplied by itself, for example, $2^3 = 2 \times 2 \times 2 = 8$. The symbols representing inequalities (> and <) are used in problems and for the purpose of representing values on a number line.

Get familiar with the use of exponents by practicing problems that use them on a frequent basis. Ask your child to explain what an exponent indicates and support him in explaining that the exponent tells you how many times a number should be multiplied by itself.

## Geometry

Students find the area and volume of shapes and are also asked to draw shapes in the coordinate plane for the purpose of finding the length of sides.

Continue to practice finding the area and volume of shapes on paper or by measuring objects around your home environment and applying the formulas for area and volume.

## Statistics and probability

Students explore the purpose and use of statistics and identify situations that involve the need for data collection because the characteristics of a population will vary. When looking at collected data, they must be able to display data in various ways (such as on graphs and charts) and make determinations about the distribution of data as it relates to the similarities and differences in the population.

Reinforce your child's grasp of statistics by collecting some data of your own. Create a list of choices, such as colors or ice-cream flavors, and let your child poll friends and/or family members. Then she can make a visual representation on paper or in a computer spreadsheet and draw conclusions about the preferences of the people (or population) represented in the poll.

# Solving Real-World Problems Involving Fractions, Ratios, and More in Grade 7

In Grade 7, students use fractions to solve real-world problems involving ratios and unit rates — for example, using a fraction of a cup of seasoning per pound of meat cooked. The rules of operations are applied to negative numbers. Students incorporate more characteristics and properties of geometric shapes, such as angle measurements and circumference, as a means of describing shapes, while their use of statistics explores the process of making generalizations about a population.

## Ratios and proportional relationships

Fractions are used in ratios, including the unit and rate. Students begin to identify proportional relationships and to describe the relationships that exist, such as percentages used in sales. They use tables and graphs to represent ratios and solve multistep problems involving real-world applications such as calculating tips and interest.

Build on your child's understanding of ratios by looking at circumstances that involve a fraction. When cooking, encourage your child to predict which recipe will be saltier: a recipe that uses ¾ tablespoon of salt per three pounds or a second recipe that uses ½ tablespoon per two pounds. (These ratios are equivalent and use the same amount of salt per pound.)

## The number system

Students continue to build their understanding of rational numbers and absolute value. They represent addition and subtraction on a number line and understand that subtracting a positive number from another positive number results in the same movement on the number line as when a negative number is added to a positive number. Students also use the rules for multiplying and dividing negative numbers with or by positive numbers and fractions.

Practice adding and subtracting negative numbers so that your child gains a sense of familiarity with the rules for sign change. Using a number line can help your child visualize addition or subtraction as a value moving up or down the number line.

## Expressions and equations

Students rewrite and solve equations and expressions with a *coefficient*, which is the number alongside a variable that's used for multiplication. For example, in the expression $3a$, 3 is the coefficient and is used to multiply the value of $a$ by 3. Real-world problems that include several steps reinforce students' previous understanding of equations and inequalities, and students actually use them to solve problems.

Reinforce the meaning of a coefficient by writing several terms that include coefficients, such as $2a$ or $5a$ (but remember that the variable $a$ can be any letter). Have your child write out how many $a$'s there would be for each term. For example, $2a = a + a$, and $5a = a + a + a + a + a$. After he gets a handle on this, add another term to the problem and make an equation such as $5a + 2 = 12$ and let him solve to find the value of $a$.

## Geometry

In Grade 7, students begin to use drawings to solve problems, including those that involve the lengths of sides and the size of angles. Students find the circumference (distance around the outside) of a circle and solve multistep problems using supplementary, complementary, vertical, and adjacent angles.

First use the formula for circumference (3.14 × the diameter of the circle) to complete simple problems on paper. Expand your child's understanding of circumference by measuring circular objects around the house and calculating the circumference.

## Statistics and probability

Students use the statistical method of sampling (gathering and analyzing data from a small subset of a population) to make generalizations about a larger population. This allows them to compare and contrast groups efficiently while also considering the degree of variability (difference) in certain populations. They also explore probability and ways to express the likelihood of an event occurring.

Find the results of national polls and figure out the number of people actually included in the polls (the sample). Reinforce your child's understanding of why samples are used in statistics. Ask your child if the population polled truly represents the larger population and discuss any problems that might arise when choosing participants.

# Gearing Up for Higher Math in Grade 8

In Grade 8, students get more comfortable with the use of rational and irrational numbers. A *rational number* is one that can be expressed as a simple fraction. An *irrational number* has no fractional equivalent; for example, the value of pi (3.1415926535897. . .) can't be expressed as 3 along with a fraction. Students are also introduced to several new concepts and skills, including the following:

- ✔ **The relationship between exponents and radicals:** While an *exponent* tells you how many times to multiply a number by itself, a *radical*, also referred to as a *root*, tells you how many times to divide a number by itself; for example, the square root of 4 is 2, because 2 × 2 = 4. The cube root of 27 is 3, because 3 × 3 × 3 = 27.

- ✔ **Functions:** *Functions* are rules that define the output for any given input; for example $y = x + 2$ is a rule that defines the value of *y* in terms of the value of *x*. If you know that *x* is 3, then you know that *y* is 5 because the rule says that 2 must be added to any input.

- ✔ **Analyzing two- and three-dimensional objects:** Students use distance, angle, and similarity to analyze shapes. They're also introduced to the *Pythagorean theorem*: the rule that in a right triangle (a triangle with a 90 degree angle), the square of the *hypotenuse* (longest side) is equal to the sum of the squares of the two other sides.

Significant emphasis is placed on the skills that prepare students for high school algebra.

## The number system

In Grade 8, students discover the difference between rational and irrational numbers and are asked to put irrational numbers on a number line as accurately as possible to the nearest rational numbers. This enables students to compare the values of multiple irrational numbers to rational numbers.

Review the difference between rational and irrational numbers and then move on to placing these numbers on a number line. Find the approximate value of an irrational number in relation to rational numbers on the number line by rounding to a specified digit (you can start simply with whole numbers and then move on to rounding to the tenths, hundredths, and thousandths place). For example, if you ask your child to round to the tenths place, pi can be rounded to 3.1, and the square root of 2 can be rounded to 1.4. Place the answers on a number line so she can see the relationship between the irrational number and its relative placement on a number line.

# Expressions and equations

Students use expressions and equations with exponents (for example, the number 2 in $4^2$) and radicals ($\sqrt{\ }$) when using square roots and cube roots or solving problems written in scientific notation. A significant aspect of this domain in Grade 8 is solving *linear equations* (an equation that results in a straight line when graphed), including the use of graphing.

Practice graphing linear equations. Create a simple coordinate plane, and remember to make sure that the equation results in graphing a straight line. For the most part, you can write linear equations by avoiding the use of exponents or radicals.

# Functions

Functions play a big role in Grade 8. Students get comfortable with how functions work by representing them with numbers, in tables, and on graphs.

Practice writing various functions and talking through the input and output. For example, $f(x) = x + 1$ indicates that the function is adding the number 1 to any value substituted for $x$. So if the number 2 takes the place of $x$, the output is 3. If the input is 5, the output is 6.

# Geometry

Students look at geometric shapes and determine whether they're *congruent* (the same size and shape) using various movements, tools, and methods. They use the Pythagorean theorem ($a^2 + b^2 = c^2$) to find the length of unknown sides of right triangles and explore its application in real-world settings.

Draw several right triangles and label two of the three sides with a number. Challenge your child to use the Pythagorean theorem to find the length of the side that's missing a value.

# Statistics and probability

Sets of data that include two variables (bivariate) require students to explore different ways of interpreting data, specifically using scatterplots. Students interpret and explain information gathered and use it to draw conclusions.

# Chapter 6

# Graduating to High School Math Standards

## In This Chapter

▶ Seeing numbers and quantities in a whole new way

▶ Using algebra to solve for unknown values

▶ Exploring mathematical relationships through functions

▶ Solving real-world problems with modeling and geometry

▶ Guesstimating with statistics and probability

The Common Core Standards for high-school math address six major domains and are organized differently than the standards in kindergarten through Grade 8. Instead of being listed by grade level, the high-school math standards are organized only by domain in order to give schools and teachers the flexibility to structure their math courses in ways they deem most effective in helping their students achieve the standards. The Common Core Standards for high-school math are as follows:

✔ Number and Quantity

✔ Algebra

✔ Functions

✔ Modeling

✔ Geometry

✔ Statistics and Probability

In this chapter, I describe each of these domains and provide examples of applications of these skills and concepts that you can use to better understand what your child is doing in school and to help reinforce your child's understanding and abilities.

You don't need to be a math whiz to help your child at home. By understanding the expectations established within each domain, monitoring your child's performance, and teaming up with teachers to address any issues and concerns regarding your child's progress, you can help keep your child on track.

# Revisiting Number and Quantity

From kindergarten through high school, students explore the concepts and application of number and quantity:

- **Number:** In K–8, students gradually increase their knowledge and skills in understanding and performing calculations with real numbers — whole numbers (counting numbers) and fractions. In Grade 8, the focus is on the difference between rational and irrational numbers — numbers that can and can't be expressed as fractions. In high school, students are ready to tackle complex or imaginary numbers. (I explain real numbers, rational and irrational numbers, and complex or imaginary numbers in the sections that follow.)

- **Quantity:** In K–8, students measure and perform calculations using simple measures, including length, width, area, and volume. High-school math challenges students to deal with increasingly complex notions of quantity that are often used in real-world applications, such as mortality rates, currency conversions, compounding interest, and acceleration.

In the following sections, I break down the high-school number and quantity standards into four groups of standards:

- The real number system
- Quantities
- The complex number system
- Vector and matrix quantities

I also explain what your child is expected to know (upon graduation) in each group and provide guidance on what you can do at home to help your child meet expectations.

The math standards for Grades 9–12 include some very complex concepts and accompanying vocabulary. I'll help you unpack some of this terminology along the way, but for more specific assistance you can reference the mathematics glossary provided at www.corestandards.org.

## The real number system

The *real number system* contains all numbers that can be represented on a number line (see Figure 6-1), including rational and irrational numbers:

- *Rational numbers* are whole numbers and fractions. You'll encounter rational numbers in various decimal forms. Even though a *repeating decimal* (such 0.33333333. . .) may not look rational, it can still be written as the fraction ⅓. *Terminating decimals,* such as 0.25, are also rational and can be written as a fraction (in this case, ¼. Students encounter rational numbers starting in kindergarten.

- *Irrational numbers* can't be written as a fraction or a ratio. You'll frequently see irrational numbers in decimal forms that can't be written as fractions. For example, pi (3.14159. . .) is an irrational number that is non-repeating but also can't be expressed as a fraction. Students begin working with irrational numbers in Grade 8.

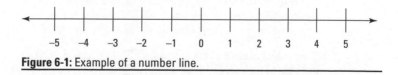

**Figure 6-1:** Example of a number line.

In high school, students begin to extend the properties of exponents (see Chapter 5) to rational exponents. By graduation, students are expected to:

- Understand and explain how the properties of integer (whole number) exponents extend to all rational exponents, including fractional exponents, such as $125^{1/3}$

✔ Express radicals in terms of rational exponents. For example:

$$\sqrt[4]{16} = 16^{1/4} \text{ and } \sqrt[3]{27} = 27^{1/3}$$

By graduation, high-school students must also be able to explain the properties of irrational numbers and why

✔ Adding two rational numbers results in a rational number.

✔ Multiplying two rational numbers results in a rational number.

✔ Adding two irrational numbers results in an irrational number.

✔ Multiplying a nonzero rational number with an irrational number results in an irrational number; for example, if $\pi$ is irrational, explain why $2\pi$ is irrational.

One of the best ways to learn anything is to try to teach it. When your child is working with rational and irrational numbers, ask her to define each term and explain the difference. After making sure that your child has an accurate understanding of these concepts, write out five or six numbers and let her identify which ones are rational and which ones are irrational. Be sure to include examples of the various types of decimals I refer to earlier in this section.

## *Quantity*

In high-school math, quantity focuses on the student's ability to reason qualitatively and use units to solve problems. For example, the student should be able to do the following:

✔ Read a multistep word problem and use units to figure out the solution. In other words, in word problems that contain values in different units (for example, distance in meters and kilometers), the student should be able to determine the most efficient conversion to use to convert all distance measurements to kilometers or meters and to solve the problem.

✔ Determine which quantities to use for descriptive modeling, for example, which units are most appropriate for solving a problem that asks for the time required to fill a swimming pool with water.

✔ Choose a level of accuracy based on measurement limitations; in other words, how precise should you be when rounding numbers up or down? For example, if you fill your gas tank with 10.275 gallons of gas priced at $3.339 dollars per gallon, the cost is $34.308225, but because you're paying with dollars and cents, rounding up to the nearest hundredth makes sense; the cost is $34.31.

✔ Choose and interpret the *origin* (the point from which data is measured) and *scale* (the tick marks along the *X* and *Y* axes) in graphic representations of data (see Figure 6-2).

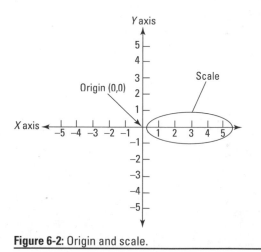

**Figure 6-2:** Origin and scale.

Challenge your child to solve real-world problems that involve several steps and various units of measure and show you how she figured it out. For example, suppose Aunt Sally is planning to meet you for lunch. The restaurant is 5 miles from her house and 15 miles from yours. Aunt Sally is leaving her home at 11:30 and will be driving an average of 30 miles an hour. You'll be driving an average of 45 miles an hour. When do you need to leave home to arrive at the restaurant five minutes before Aunt Sally?

Of course, most problems have more than one solution even though they have only one correct answer. Here's one solution: First figure out how long it takes Aunt Sally to drive to the restaurant. She's driving 30 miles per hour, so for every hour she drives, she goes 30 miles. There are 60 minutes in an hour, so to find out the number of minutes it takes Aunt Sally to drive 5 miles:

$$\frac{1\cancel{k}}{30m}\times\frac{60\min}{1\cancel{k}}=\frac{60\min}{30m}=\frac{2\min}{m}$$

$$5\cancel{m}\times\frac{2\min}{\cancel{m}}=10\min$$

Aunt Sally will arrive at the restaurant at 11:30 + 10 minutes = 11:40. You want to arrive five minutes before that at 11:35, so what time do you need to leave the house?

Perform the same calculations to determine how many minutes it takes you to drive 15 miles:

$$\frac{1\cancel{k}}{45m}\times\frac{60\min}{1\cancel{k}}=\frac{60\min}{45m}=\frac{4\min}{3m}$$

$$15\cancel{m}\times\frac{4\min}{3\cancel{m}}=\frac{60\min}{3}=20\min$$

So you need to leave your house at 11:35 − 20 minutes = 11:15.

## *The complex number system*

The *complex number system* includes both real and imaginary numbers. An imaginary number, represented as *i,* is the square root of −1; *i* is imaginary because no number multiplied by itself results in a negative value. In Grade 11, students encounter imaginary numbers as a translation on the imaginary plane. Here's what students need to know and be able to do when dealing with the complex number system:

✓ Explain what a complex (imaginary) number is:

- $i=\sqrt{-1}$

- $i^2=-1$

- *a* + *bi* = a complex number, with both *a* and *b* being real numbers

✓ Add, subtract, and multiply complex numbers using the commutative, associative, and distributive properties:

- *Commutative* enables you to add or multiply numbers in any order, for example 4 + 2 = 2 + 4

- *Associative* means you can add or multiply numbers in any grouping, for example (3 × 5) × 4 = 3 × (5 × 4)

- *Distributive* is commonly represented as

  a × (b + c) = (a × b) + (a × c)

So, students should be able to solve equations such as:

$$
\begin{aligned}
(5-7i)(-3+5i) &= 5(-3+5i) = -7i(-3+5i) \\
&= -15+25i+21i-35i^2 \\
&= -15+i(25+21)-35i^2 \\
&= -15+46i-35i^2 \\
&= -15+46i-35(-1) \\
&= -15+46i+35 \\
&= 20+46i
\end{aligned}
$$

✔ Find the conjugate of a complex number and use conjugates to find moduli and quotients of complex numbers. A *conjugate* is a *binomial expression* (representing the sum or difference of two terms) formed by negating the second term of a binomial; for example, the conjugate of a + b is a – b.

✔ When an imaginary number is involved, you have a *complex conjugate*; for example, in the expression $m = a + bi$ the complex conjugate represented is $\bar{m} = a - bi$.

A sample problem may provide a given and ask you to use the conjugate to find the modulus and quotient; for example, given that $y = 3 - 7i$ and $z = 5 + 2i$, find the modulus of $y$ and the quotient of $z$ and $y$:

To find the modulus of $y$ using its complex conjugate, students may solve an equation like the following:

$$
\begin{aligned}
|y|^2 &= y\bar{y} \\
&= (3-7i)(3+7i) \\
&= 9+21i-21i-49i^2 \\
&= 9-49i^2 \\
&= 9-49(-1) \\
&= 9+49 \\
&= 58
\end{aligned}
$$

$$
|y| = \sqrt{58}
$$

As you can see, you use the distributive property to multiply the two binomials in the first step. You can use the FOIL method (first terms, outside terms, inside terms, last terms) to remember how to do this: first ($3 \times 3$), outside ($3 \times 7i$), inside ($-7i \times 3$), and last ($-7i \times 7i$). After multiplying these terms, you arrive at a polynomial with four terms. Then you combine like terms (any terms with the same variable, in this case $21i$ and $-21i$) and complete any remaining operations. Because $i$ is the square root of $-1$, you can change $i^2$ into $-1$ and multiply it by $-49$, resulting in changing it to a positive number. After calculating $9 + 49 = 58$, take the square root of 58 because you're solving for $y^2$ and want to find $y$ instead.

To find the quotient of $z$ and $y$:

$$\frac{z}{y} = \frac{5+2i}{3-7i}$$

$$= \frac{5+2i}{3-7i} \times \frac{3+7i}{3+7i}$$

$$= \frac{15+35i+6i+14i^2}{9+21i-21i-25i^2}$$

$$= \frac{15+41i+14(-1)}{9-25(-1)}$$

$$= \frac{1+41i}{16}$$

✔ Represent complex numbers on the complex plane in rectangular and polar form and explain why the rectangular and polar forms of a complex number represent the same number. In the complex plane, the horizontal axis ($X$) represents real numbers, and the vertical axis ($Yi$) represents imaginary numbers. Imaginary numbers can be represented on the complex plane in two forms:

- **Rectangular form:** The intersection of the real and imaginary numbers is shown as the intersection of coordinates on the $X$ and $Yi$ axes. Figure 6-3 shows $4 + 3i$ graphed in rectangular form.

- **Polar form:** The real number represents the vector length (how far the vector reaches into the imaginary plane), and $\theta$ represents the angle the vector forms with the real axis (the familiar axis represented by $x$ and $y$). Polar form is derived from the Pythagorean theorem, $r^2 = a^2 + b^2$. The actual conversion is beyond the scope of this book, but it provides the length of the hypotenuse of a triangle along with one angle, which provides sufficient data to plot the value in the complex plane. Figure 6-4 shows $4 + 3i$ graphed in polar form.

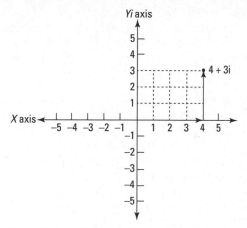

**Figure 6-3:** 4 + 3i graphed in rectangular form.

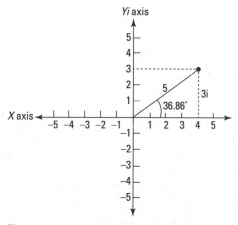

**Figure 6-4:** 4 + 3i graphed in polar form.

✔ Represent addition, subtraction, multiplication, and conjugation on the complex plane.

✔ Solve *quadratic equations* (equations in which the highest power of an unknown is a square) with real coefficients that have complex solutions. For example, students may be asked to solve $x^2 + 2x = 0$ over complex numbers.

✔ Extend polynomial identities to complex numbers. For example, $x + 7$ using complex numbers can be expressed as $(x + 7i) \times (x - 7i)$.

✔ Grasp the *Fundamental Theorem of Algebra*, which states that any polynomial of $n$ degree has $n$ *roots* (places where the polynomial is equal to zero when graphed). For example, in a polynomial with one variable, such as $5x^6 + 8x - 2$, the $n$ degree is 6, so the polynomial has 6 roots.

As you can see, the complex number system earns its name in more ways than one. The introduction to vectors I provide in this section will be used later when students get into higher mathematics. You can support your child at home by showing interest; monitoring progress; encouraging your child to seek help, if necessary; and expressing any concerns you have to your child's math teacher. You can also track down websites that can help you understand these concepts. Visit www. khanacademy.org and www.illustrativemathematics. org for more examples and explanations.

## Vector and matrix quantities

Rounding out a high-school student's understanding of quantity are vector and matrix quantities, as I explain in the following sections.

### Exploring vector quantities

A *vector* is any quantity that has magnitude and direction. For example, *velocity*, which is the rate of change in the position of an object, is a vector because it describes the speed and direction in which the object moves. Speed, on the other hand, is not a vector, because it indicates only how fast an object is going, not its direction.

High-school math introduces students to vectors. Initially, students discover what vector quantities are and how to represent them using directed line segments, as shown in Figure 6-5. Note that the length of the line segment indicates its relative magnitude, while the orientation of the line segment indicates its direction.

Common Core Standards for vector quantities become increasingly demanding. Upon graduation, students should be able to

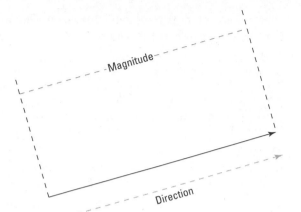

**Figure 6-5:** A vector is a quantity that has magnitude and direction.

✔ Use special notation to indicate vector magnitude and direction:

- Vertical lines on either side of a number indicate vector magnitude, for example |v| (or ||v|| to distinguish vector magnitude from absolute value).

- Coordinates are often used to specify the start and end points of a vector and define both its direction and magnitude; for example, (0,0) (3,4) describes a vector that starts where the $X$ and $Y$ axes cross and points up and to the right to where $X = 3$ and $Y = 4$. Using the Pythagorean theorem, you can calculate the magnitude of the line as

$$c = \sqrt{3^2 + 4^2}$$
$$= \sqrt{9 + 16}$$
$$= \sqrt{25}$$
$$= 5$$

✔ Subtract the coordinates of a vector's initial and terminal points to find the vector's components — the two sides of the imaginary triangle that define the vector (the hypotenuse of the triangle); for example, for a vector (−3,0) and (5,3), the components of the vector are 5 − (−3) = 8 and 3 − 0 = 3.

✔ Use vectors to solve problems involving velocity and other vector qualities; for example, a question may ask how long it would take you to canoe across a river if you average 10 meters per second with no current, and the river is flowing at 5 meters per second.

✔ Add vectors by placing them end to end, using their components, or following the parallelogram rule, as shown in Figure 6-6. According to the parallelogram rule, you can determine the sum of two vectors by placing them head to tail and drawing a vector from the free tail to the free head.

✔ Subtract one vector from another. To subtract vectors, reverse the direction of the vector you want to subtract and then add them as you normally would.

✔ Multiply a vector by a *scalar* — a real number that changes the vector's magnitude, direction, or both:

- Multiplying a vector by a positive number other than 1 changes only its magnitude.

- Multiplying a vector by –1 reverses its direction but doesn't alter its magnitude.

- Multiplying a vector by a negative number other than –1 reverses the direction and changes the magnitude.

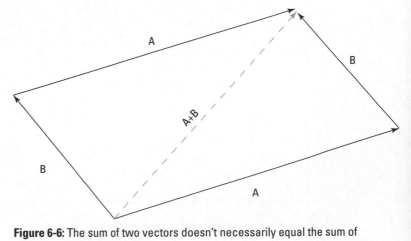

**Figure 6-6:** The sum of two vectors doesn't necessarily equal the sum of their magnitudes.

Solve the following word problem: A plane flies due south at 100 miles per hour. The wind is blowing 25 miles per hour from the west. In what direction and how far will the plane fly in one hour?

Drawing a picture helps determine the equation needed to solve this problem (see Figure 6-7).

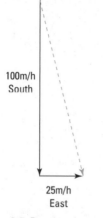

100m/h
South

25m/h
East

**Figure 6-7:** Draw a picture to envision the situation described in the word problem.

Use the Pythagorean theorem to solve the problem:

$$100^2 + 25^2 = c^2$$

$$c = \sqrt{100^2 + 25^2} = \sqrt{10000 + 625} = \sqrt{10625} \cong 103.1$$

So the answer is that the plane flies southeast 103.1 miles (rounded up to the nearest tenth).

### Investigating matrix quantities

A *matrix* is a set of numbers arranged in columns and rows, as shown here.

$$\begin{bmatrix} 25 & 16 & 84 & 73 & 32 \\ 7 & 14 & 28 & 35 & 46 \\ 29 & 32 & 77 & 58 & 39 \\ 18 & 74 & 53 & 90 & 46 \end{bmatrix}$$

Students begin to use matrices to analyze data and perform calculations, including multiplication with scalars and other matrices. Mastery of matrices is demonstrated by an ability to

✔ Create a matrix to represent data. For example, a teacher has three classes of students. Grade distributions for Class 1 are 4 A's, 9 B's, 15 C's, 3 D's, and 2 F's. Grade distributions for Class 2 are 6 A's, 7 B's, 10 C's, 4 D's, and 1 F. For Class 3, grade distributions are 3 A's, 12 B's, 11 C's, 2 D's, and 2 F's. The matrix looks like this:

|         | A | B  | C  | D | F |
|---------|---|----|----|---|---|
| Class 1 | 4 | 9  | 15 | 3 | 2 |
| Class 2 | 6 | 7  | 10 | 4 | 1 |
| Class 3 | 3 | 12 | 11 | 2 | 2 |

✔ Multiply a matrix by a scalar. For example, if a company sells 200 of product X, 250 of product Y, and 300 of product Z in the United States and 150 of product X, 275 of product Y, and 325 of product Z in China and it expects to triple sales in both countries the following year, how much of each product does the company need to manufacture?

In this problem the scalar is 3, so you multiply it by each number in the matrix and then add the resulting numbers for products X, Y, and Z:

$$3 \times [200 \quad 250 \quad 300] = [600 \quad 750 \quad 900]$$

✔ Determine whether two matrices can be added, subtracted, or multiplied and, if they can be, perform the designated operation.

• Matrices can be added or subtracted only if they have the same number of columns and rows. You can then add or subtract the corresponding numbers in the two matrices and simplify.

• Matrices can be multiplied only if the number of rows in one matrix equals the number of columns in the other matrix. You can then multiply the rows of the first matrix by the columns of the second.

A candy store charges by the pound $6 for taffy, $5 for gumdrops, and $10 for caramel corn. Weekly sales for each in pounds during March are:

|              | Week 1 | Week 2 | Week 3 | Week 4 |
|--------------|--------|--------|--------|--------|
| **Taffy**        | 4      | 9      | 7      | 8      |
| **Gumdrops**     | 8      | 7      | 9      | 10     |
| **Caramel corn** | 10     | 8      | 9      | 7      |

Using matrices, determine total sales in dollars per week.

$$\begin{bmatrix} \$6 & \$5 & \$10 \end{bmatrix} \times \begin{bmatrix} 4 & 9 & 7 & 8 \\ 8 & 7 & 9 & 10 \\ 10 & 8 & 9 & 7 \end{bmatrix} =$$

$$(\$6\times4)+(\$5\times8)+(\$10\times10) = \$24+\$40+\$100 = \$164$$

$$(\$6\times9)+(\$5\times7)+(\$10\times8) = \$54+\$35+\$80 = \$169$$

$$(\$6\times7)+(\$5\times9)+(\$10\times9) = \$42+\$45+\$90 = \$177$$

$$(\$6\times8)+(\$5\times10)+(\$10\times7) = \$48+\$50+\$70 = \$168$$

|           | Week 1 | Week 2 | Week 3 | Week 4 |
|-----------|--------|--------|--------|--------|
| **Total** | $164   | $169   | $177   | $168   |

In this example, the price for each different type of candy is multiplied by the amount of candy sold during each week. This occurs by multiplying the prices ($6, $5, or $10) by the amounts indicated in the matrix. The vertical rows represent the total amount of candy sold in an individual week, while the horizontal rows represent the total amount of a specific type of candy sold each week over four total weeks.

To solve this problem, you multiply the price for a specific kind of candy by the amount of that type of candy sold each week (the horizontal rows). After doing that for all three types of candy, add the product for each type of candy to determine the amount of money earned each week.

# Discovering the Unknowns with Algebra

Algebra is a branch of mathematics that uses letters and other symbols in equations to represent unknown values and then uses what is known to figure out what is unknown. For example, if $5x = 40$ (that is, 5 multiplied by $x$ equals 40), you know that $x = 8$ because given what we've been told — the known information — 5 is the only number that makes the number sentence true (5 × 8 = 40). In the following sections, I explain the key concepts and skills that are the focus of the Common Core Standards in algebra.

## Spotting structure in expressions

A major emphasis is on interpretation of the parts of an expression, such as coefficients and terms. In math, a *coefficient* is the number place before a variable (so in $4x$, 4 is the coefficient and $x$ is the variable). A *term* can be a single number, a variable, or a coefficient and variable together. Understanding the interaction of coefficients and variables results in students being able to rewrite the expression in different ways, which requires an understanding of each part of the expression and of how all of the parts of an expression interact given the rules of math operations.

*Expressions* are numbers, symbols, and operators (+, −, ×, and ÷) grouped together to show value. Expressions differ from *equations*, which employ the use of an equal sign (=) to show that the values on either side of it are equal or to demonstrate the value of a variable.

Practice translating written or spoken expressions into numerical expressions for use in calculations. For example, you can write the statement "2 less than 5 times a number" as the expression $5x - 2$. If $x = 7$, then $5(7) - 2 = 35 - 2 = 33$.

## Grasping polynomials and rational expressions

Students start to work with *polynomials*, which are expressions that have more than one variable. They use addition, subtraction, multiplication, and division with polynomials.

Students are also introduced to the concept of factoring to simplify expressions and solve problems. *Factoring* involves finding values that multiplied together result in the expression; for example, the expression $5x - 5$ can be factored as $5(x - 1)$ the same way that 14 can be factored as $2 \times 7$.

Write out a polynomial and have your child name the parts, as in the following example:

$$4x^2 + 5x - 3$$

This is a *trinomial* because it has three expressions linked together with operators. It's easy to get confused and count the $x$ and $x^2$ as separate entities, but in this problem they're part of the coefficients beside them. The operators (addition and subtraction signs in this problem) separate the parts of this trinomial.

The number 4 is the *leading coefficient*, $x$ is a *variable*, $^2$ is an *exponent*, and $^2$ is also the highest power in the equation. The 2 at the end is a *constant*.

Solve this problem, which involves a polynomial: If the area of a rectangle is expressed as $x^2 + 7x + 12$ and the length of one side is $x + 4$, what is the length of the other side?

To solve this problem, factor $x^2 + 7x + 12$ as $(x + 3)(x + 4)$, so the length of the other side is $(x + 3)$.

## Building equations

Students use equations to describe the relationships that exist between variables, including solving equations that are representative of real-world situations. The use of *modeling* (the application of mathematical concepts to practical situations) is a significant aspect of these standards. (For more about modeling, see "Applying Mathematics to the Real World with Modeling," later in this chapter.)

Relationships between variables involve the interaction between variables and coefficients. For example, in $3x = y$, the value of $y$ is dependent on the value of $x$. In other words, as the value of $x$ increases or decreases, so does the value of $y$.

Build an equation to solve a problem involving a real-world scenario. For example, imagine that a farmer wants to build a rectangular pen for his animals. He has 200 feet of fencing materials, and he needs one side of the rectangle to be 30 feet long. How long do the other sides need to be?

Start by drawing a rectangle and labeling the two shorter sides "30 feet." Label the two longer sides "x." (See Figure 6-8.)

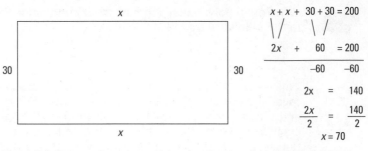

**Figure 6-8:** Draw a picture to envision the situation described in the word problem.

Represented in the form of an equation, you write: $x + x + 30 + 30 = 200$. After combining like terms, you're left with $2x + 60 = 200$. Subtract 60 from both sides of the equation, and you get $2x = 140$. Divide both sides by 2, and you have your answer: Each of the longer sides of the rectangle is 70 feet.

# Reasoning with equations and inequalities

Students solve equations by finding accurate solutions, practicing the skill of substituting numbers for variables to ensure accuracy. Checking the accuracy of an answer, including how reasonable an answer is in the context of a problem, does more to build problem-solving skills than merely having a student use an algorithm to solve equations. An *algorithm* is a step-by-step procedure to solve a problem.

Checking the accuracy of an answer is an essential skill. When solving for a variable in an equation, such as $3x + 5 = 35$, students can plug in their answer for $x$ to see if they're right. So after solving for $x$ and finding that $x$ equals 10, they plug in 10 for $x$ and do the math: $3(10) + 5 = 35$. If both sides are equal, then they solved the problem accurately.

Checking the reasonableness of an answer involves making a logical determination of whether the answer is reasonable given the context of a math problem. For example, if an object is thrown upward in the air, how long does it take for the object to hit the ground, given that $s(t) = t^2 - 2t + 35$, with $t$ representing time measured in seconds? (The $s(t)$ is function notation, as I explain in the next section. Instead of noting the function as $f(x)$, this problem indicates more specifically that seconds is a function of time.)

$$0 = -t^2 - 2t + 35$$
$$= -(t^2 + 2t - 35)$$
$$= -(t + 7)(t - 5)$$

So, $t$ can equal −7 seconds or 5 seconds. Is −7 seconds a reasonable answer? Of course not!

# Putting the "Fun" in Functions

Students become familiar with the concept of a function and the notation used with regard to functions (which is most commonly shown as $f(x)$, pronounced "eff of ex," in many problems). A *function* is a rule that dictates the output for every input. For example, $f(x) = 3x + 4$ means $x$ is always 4 more than 3 times any number. If $x$ is 2, then the output of the function is 10. If $x$ is 3, then the output of the function is 13.

Students also work with functions represented in multiple ways. One of the most basic forms is a table with inputs and outputs being listed:

| x | y |
|---|---|
| 2 | 10 |
| 3 | 13 |
| 4 | 16 |

Functions are also graphed on a coordinate plane or mapped, as shown in Figure 6-9.

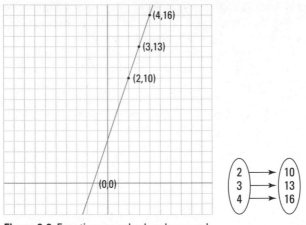

**Figure 6-9:** Functions graphed and mapped.

# Creating functions

Students create functions that represent real-world situations. They also write functions based on information given in a table or graph. For example, you may have a table with input and output values and write a function that accurately describes the relationship between two values. In creating functions, it's important that students explain the meaning of each variable used in their creation (because each variable represents a specific part of the problem).

Try to point out real-world scenarios that involve functions. For example, imagine that a plumber charges $50 as a flat fee plus $30 for each hour worked. You can write a function that demonstrates cost in terms of the hours worked by the plumber. If $c(h) = 50 + 30h$ (the cost per hour is 50 plus 30 times the number of hours worked), then 1 hour of service costs $80. This is determined by plugging in the number of hours ($h$). If the plumber works 2 hours, the total cost is $110.

# Exploring linear, quadratic, and exponential models

Students use linear models to describe natural phenomena. This is where certain entities grow at a constant rate of change. An example of this is measuring the amount of direct sunlight received during the course of a day because of the rotation of the earth.

Students work with *quadratic models*. A *quadratic* is a polynomial with the highest power being the second power.

Give it a try with the following example: Imagine a ball is thrown upward with an initial velocity of 16 feet per second from a height of 96 feet. How long does it take for the ball to hit the ground? Use this model for a free-falling object: $s(t) = -16t^2 + v_0 + s_0$ with $-16t^2$ representing gravity, $v_0$ representing initial velocity (16 feet per second), and $s_0$ representing initial height (96 feet).

To solve this problem, set the function equal to zero (0) and insert the known values into the equation:

$$s(t) = -16t^2 + 16t + 96$$
$$0 = -16t^2 + 16t + 96$$

Dividing both sides by $-16$ simplifies the equation to: $0 = t^2 - t - 6$

Factor the equation to simplify: $0 = (t-3)(t+2)$

You now know that $t$ can be 3 or $-2$. Is $-2$ reasonable? Of course not! So, the correct answer is 3.

Students solve problems with exponential models. An *exponential model* is a function with a variable as the exponent. An example is $5^{.02x}$. With exponential models, the function is growing at a percent rate — in this example, the rate is .02, or 2 percent. Examples of exponential phenomena are interest, half-life, and population models.

Try it out with this example using a formula for interest that is compounded continuously: $A = Pe^{rt}$. In this formula, $A$ is the amount earned over time, $P$ is the initial investment, $e$ is known as Euler's number and has an approximate value of 2.718, $r$ is the interest rate, and $t$ is time. How long will it take $2,000 invested at 5 percent interest to double if the interest is compounded continuously?

Euler's number, $e$, is used in math for purposes of calculating quantities (such as interest) that continuously compound. Because Euler's number is an irrational number, all you need to know is the circumstances in which it would be used, not the number itself.

To solve this problem, start by writing the equation using your known values:

$$\$4000 = \$2000e^{.05t}$$

Divide both sides by $2,000 to simplify:

$$\frac{\$4000}{\$2000} = \frac{\$2000e^{.05t}}{\$2000}$$
$$2 = e^{.05t}$$

In many equations, students use inverse operations to find the value of certain variables. The inverse of addition is subtraction. The inverse of multiplication is division. You're most likely comfortable with using these operations in equations. Although Euler's number ($e$) may be a new concept for you, using the inverse operation is easy. When you want to cancel out $e$, all you have to do is multiply both sides by the natural log (ln). You should be able to find this button or feature on most graphing and scientific calculators.

To further simplify, eliminate $e$ by multiplying both sides by the natural log (ln), which is the inverse of $e$; multiplying any number by its inverse gives you 1:

$$2 = e^{.05t}$$
$$\ln 2 = \ln e^{.05t}$$
$$\ln 2 = .05t \ln e$$
$$\ln 2 = .05t$$
$$\frac{\ln 2}{.05} = \frac{.05t}{.05}$$
$$t = \frac{\ln 2}{.05}$$

At this point, you need to get out your handy-dandy calculator to do the math. The calculator tells you that ln2 equals approximately .693. Divide that by .05 and you get approximately 13.86 years.

# Working with trigonometric functions

Students extend their knowledge of trigonometric ratios in relation to right triangles to angles greater than 90 degrees. Trigonometric functions are used in right triangles as ratios that are formed by two different sides of the triangle. (For more about trigonometric ratios, see "Similarity, right triangles, and trigonometry," later in this chapter.)

Students use trigonometric ratios to model periodic natural phenomena such as the motion of a pendulum, the height of waves, and monthly temperatures over the course of time. Students also prove previously learned trigonometric identities.

If the average temperature in a city for each month is given by $t = 1$ representing January 15, $t = 2$ representing February 15, and so on, you can find the temperature of September 15 by using a trigonometric function. Assume that the average monthly temperature for the city is 54.4, with the highest monthly average being 76.9 (54.4 + 22.5) and the lowest monthly average being 31.9 (54.4 − 22.5).

To solve this problem, start with the equation $y = a\sin(bx + c) + d$, where $a$ is amplitude, $b$ is period (in this case 2π/12 or π/6), $x$ is $t$ (time), and $d$ is average temperature. Now, plug in the known values to get

$$y = 22.5\sin(\frac{\pi t}{6} - 2) + 54.4$$

Replace $t$ with 9 because September is the ninth month:

$$y = 22.5\sin(\frac{\pi 9}{6} - 2) + 54.4$$

Finally, use your calculator (in radian mode) to crunch the numbers:

$$y = 22.5\sin\left(\frac{3.14159 \times 9}{6} - 2\right) + 54.4$$
$$= 22.5\sin\left(\frac{28.27}{6} - 2\right) + 54.4$$
$$= 22.5\sin(4.7124 - 2) + 54.4$$
$$= 22.5\sin(2.7124) + 54.4$$
$$= 22.5 \times (.41614) + 54.4$$
$$= 9.36 + 54.4 = 63.76°$$

# Applying Mathematics to the Real World with Modeling

The emphasis on modeling in the high-school math classroom is to ensure that students can apply learned concepts in math to real-world applications. This moves the use of math from abstract theory into useful practice. Although you won't find any additional content in the section on modeling standards, the purpose of the math standards is to help students apply the skills and concepts learned throughout their time in school. The standards include guidance on which standards should be used for modeling by identifying them with a star symbol (*).

# Shaping Up with Geometry

*Geometry* is a branch of mathematics that explores the nature and properties of points, lines, planes, and a host of shapes, including rectangles, triangles, circles, and spheres. In the following sections, I introduce the Common Core Standards that apply to geometry.

## Congruence

Students show that two shapes are *congruent*, indicating that all sides and angles of the shape are exactly the same. Students also use rigid motions to move one shape on top of another to show that all parts are the same. *Rigid motions* involve moving an object without changing its size or shape.

Take a look at the example of rigid motion (reflection and translation in this instance) in the coordinate plane, as shown in Figure 6-10. Notice that the size of the shape hasn't changed even though it is reflected over to the left and translated down.

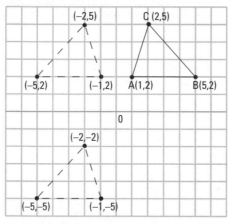

**Figure 6-10:** Rigid motion is the moving of shapes without changing their dimensions.

# Similarity, right triangles, and trigonometry

The Common Core Standards in this group focus primarily on triangles. Students discover the concept of similarity and scale and explore how these concepts apply to real-world situations. The unique nature of triangles also reveals certain mathematical truths about ratios that are very useful in solving a host of problems.

## Similarity

In geometry, *similarity* refers to triangles that have exactly the same shape but differ in size. Similarity differs from *congruence*, which describes triangles of identical size and shape. The use of similarity to represent larger objects is commonplace in fields such as engineering and architecture, when someone needs to accurately represent the size of certain objects on a smaller scale.

## Right triangles

Students work extensively with right triangles (triangles with one 90-degree angle). Right triangles are unique in that you can find the length of any one side of the triangle if you know the lengths of the other two sides. According to the Pythagorean theorem, "the square of the hypotenuse is equal to the sum of the squares of the other two sides," which can be expressed as $c^2 = a^2 + b^2$, where $c$ is the hypotenuse (the longest side of the right triangle), and $a$ and $b$ are the other two (shorter) sides.

## Trigonometry

*Trigonometry* deals with the study and use of ratios involving triangle sides and angles. Students use the trigonometric ratios sine (sin), cosine (cos), and tangent (tan) to solve for missing parts (including a missing side or angle) of a right triangle:

$$\sin(\theta) = \frac{Opposite}{Hypotenuse}$$

$$\cos(\theta) = \frac{Adjacent}{Hypotenuse}$$

$$\tan(\theta) = \frac{Opposite}{Adjacent}$$

Using trigonometric ratios, you can determine the length of a side of a right triangle without knowing the lengths of the other two sides. You can determine the unknown length of a side given the length of one side and the angle next to it, for example. Table 6-1 indicates in which situations you use sine, cosine, and tangent. Take a look at the triangles in Figure 6-11 for a visual representation of the opposite, adjacent, and hypotenuse sides when labeled for the purposes of practicing using these ratios.

### Table 6-1 Know when to use sine, cosine, and tangent

| Use | To find | Given |
|---|---|---|
| sine | opposite | angle & hypotenuse |
| | hypotenuse | angle & opposite |
| | angle | opposite and hypotenuse |
| cosine | hypotenuse | angle & adjacent |
| | adjacent | angle & hypotenuse |
| | angle | adjacent & opposite |

| Use | To find | Given |
|---|---|---|
| tangent | opposite | angle & adjacent |
| | adjacent | angle & opposite |
| | angle | opposite & adjacent |

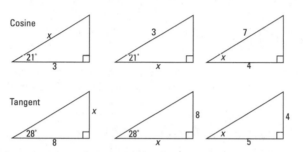

**Figure 6-11:** Challenge your child to choose the correct ratio and find the missing parts.

Draw right triangles in various sizes and dimensions that have different missing parts and have your child use the trigonometric ratios of sine, cosine, and tangent to find the missing angle or side of each triangle. Figure 6-11 shows some examples grouped by cosine, sine, and tangent, but don't tell your child which ratio to use; challenge her to figure it out.

For example, to find $x$ (opposite side) of the triangle in the upper left, knowing the angle is $19°$ and the hypotenuse is 4, you use the sine function:

$$\sin\theta = \frac{opposite}{hypotenuse}$$

$$\sin 19° = \frac{x}{4}$$

$$4 \times \sin 19° = x$$

$$x = 4 \times .326 = 1.304$$

Being able to accurately determine the missing side or angle of a right triangle is important because of the frequency of right triangles in the real world, including square objects that are divided into two right triangles and angles of elevation. Trigonometric ratios are even more useful for finding missing sides and angles of non-right *(oblique)* triangles — triangles that don't have a 90-degree angle — because the Pythagorean theorem works to find only missing sides of right triangles.

You can use the sine (sin), cosine (cos), and tangent (tan) buttons on your child's calculator when working problems that require the use of any of these trigonometric ratios.

## Circles

Common Core Standards require that upon graduation students know circles inside and out. Expectations include the following:

✔ Explain why all circles are similar.

✔ Draw inscribed angles, radii, tangents, and chords and explain how they're related (see Figure 6-12).

✔ Know that a circle's radius is perpendicular to the tangent at the point where the radius touches the circle.

✔ Find the area of any given *sector* of a circle (to envision a *sector*, imagine a slice cut out of a round pizza).

✔ Find the length of an *arc* on the perimeter of a circle (the length of the curved side of a sector). (High-school students already know how to find the *circumference* — the length all the way around a circle.)

Draw a circle with a radius of six inches, with a sector that has an interior angle of 45 degrees, and ask your child to calculate the area of the sector. You'll need to use a compass and protractor to be precise with your measurements.

The formula for the area of the entire circle is $A = \pi r^2$ so $A = \pi \times 6^2 = 3.14159 \times 32 = 100.53$ square inches. A circle is 360 degrees, so the area of the sector is 45/360 times the total area of the circle. The fraction 45/360 reduces to $\frac{1}{8}$, so the area of the sector is $100.53 \times \frac{1}{8} = 12.57$ rounded to the nearest hundredth.

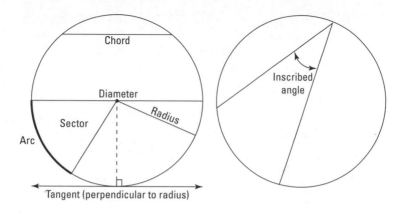

**Figure 6-12:** Parts of a circle.

Using the same circle, ask your child to find the length of the sector's arc.

To find the arc, your child must calculate the circumference of the circle and then multiply it by the same fraction: $\frac{1}{8}$. The formula for the circumference of a circle is $C = \pi d$ where $d$ is diameter. Diameter is twice the radius of 6 inches or 12 inches, so $C = \pi \times 12 = 37.70$ rounded to the nearest hundredth.

So $\frac{1}{8}$ of that is about 4.71.

## Geometric properties as equations

Students use what they know about operations in algebra to demonstrate (or prove) certain aspects or characteristics of geometric shapes. For example, if you know that the three interior angles of a triangle must add up to 180 degrees and that the first two angles are 70 and 50 degrees, you know that the third angle is $180 - 70 - 50 = 60$ degrees.

Students also begin to explore *conic sections* (or simply *conics*) — curves, circles, or ellipses formed by a plane slicing through a cone, as shown in Figure 6-13.

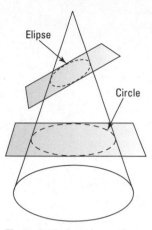

**Figure 6-13:** A conic section.

Upon graduation, students need to be able to translate between the equation and the graphical representation of conic sections.

If the center of a circle is represented by $(h, k)$ as an ordered pair, then the equation of a circle is $(x - h)^2 + (y - k)^2 = r^2$, with $r$ being the radius. For our purposes, let's say that the center of the circle is at (3, 4) and that the radius of the circle is 5. If you graph this on a coordinate plane, then all points lying on the circumference of the circle can substitute for the values of $x$ and $y$ in the equation. To test whether you've graphed the circle correctly, pick a point that you know should be on the circumference and insert it into the equation. For example, the ordered pair (8, 4) should lie on the circumference. When you substitute (8, 4) for $x$ and $y$, the equation is still true.

$$(8 - 3)^2 + (4 - 4)^2 = 25$$

$$5^2 = 25$$

The equation represents a cross section of a cone taken parallel to the base. The equation defines a circle with a center at $x = 3$, $y = 4$ and a radius of 5, as shown in Figure 6-14.

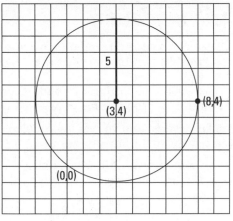

**Figure 6-14:** A circle with a center at $x = 3$, $y = 4$ and a radius of 5.

# Geometric measurement and dimension

Geometric measurement and dimension standards call on students to use formulas for the volumes of three-dimensional figures, including spheres, cones, cylinders, and pyramids:

- ✓ **Volume of a sphere:** $\frac{4}{3}\pi r^2$ where $r$ is the radius of the sphere

- ✓ **Volume of a cone:** $\frac{1}{3}\pi r^{2h}$ where $r$ is the radius of the cone's base and $h$ is its height

- ✓ **Volume of a cylinder:** $\pi r^2 h$ where $r$ is the radius of the cylinder's base and $h$ is its height

- ✓ **Volume of a pyramid:** $\frac{1}{3}bh$ where $b$ is the area of the pyramid's base and $h$ is its height

Ask your child to calculate the volume of a cylinder that's 8 centimeters in height and 10 centimeters in diameter. To solve this problem, plug the numbers into the formula for the volume of a cylinder: $\pi r^2 h = \pi \times 10^2 \times 8 = 3.14159 \times 100 \times 8 = 3.14159 \times 800 = 2513.27$ cubic centimeters.

## Geometric modeling

Modeling with geometry calls on students to apply geometric concepts to real-world situations, such as the following:

✔ Estimate the volume of an aboveground swimming pool using the formula for the volume of a cylinder.

✔ Use formulas for area and volume to calculate population density in a given environment.

✔ Design a structure using various geometric methods to achieve a specific goal, such as using the least amount of building materials.

Have your child calculate the volume or the space inside various three-dimensional objects or areas around your house. For example, you may have your child calculate the number of gallons of water your water heater holds (without peeking at the number on the water heater, of course).

# Crunching Numbers with Statistics and Probability

*Statistics* (which analyzes existing data) and *probability* (which uses existing data to predict future events) are two branches of math that students can see at work in the world. Statistics are used in everything from gauging how citizens feel about a certain politician to setting insurance premiums to informing the debate about climate change. Probability is often used to make decisions, such as when to plant a certain crop, whether a business should expand, or whether an individual should run for political office.

In the following sections, I introduce the key Common Core Standards that apply to different areas within the realm of statistics and probability.

# Interpreting categorical and quantitative data

Expectations in this area call on students to gather, analyze, and present two types of data:

 ✔ **Categorical:** Categorical data is often used to compare and contrast groups; for example, one study shows that the most popular car color is white. Silver and black are tied for second.

 ✔ **Quantitative:** Quantitative data represents measurements, such as length, number of votes, population density, and so forth.

Students display data in various forms, including number lines, graphs, and charts using various measures of the center and methods to determine patterns, repetition, and trends in data. Some common terms that you're likely to encounter are

 ✔ *mean* (the average)

 ✔ *median* (the middle number when data is organized from least to greatest)

 ✔ *standard deviation* (a description of the distance from the center in a collection of data)

 ✔ *correlation* (when the frequency or occurrence of two things is related)

 ✔ *causation* (when something causes another event to happen)

Here's an example of a typical problem that requires the use of existing data to make predictions regarding future situations: Imagine that a bank is busiest from 4 p.m. to 6 p.m. on weekday evenings. During these hours, the wait time in the drive-through is normally distributed, with a mean of 8 minutes and a standard deviation of 2 minutes. Using standard deviations, determine a) the percentage of customers who wait 10 minutes or longer, b) the percentage who wait between 4 and 12 minutes, and c) the percentage who wait 2 minutes or less.

Draw a standard bell curve, as shown in Figure 6-15, and then do the math:

a) 10 minutes or longer: Add the percentages in the 10–12, 12–14, and >14 ranges: 13.6 + 2.2 + 0.1 = 15.9 percent

b) 4 to 12 minutes: Add the percentages in the 4–6, 6–8, 8–10, and 10–12 ranges: 13.6 + 34.1 + 34.1 + 13.6 = 47.7 + 47.7 = 95.4 percent

c) Less than 2 minutes: Take the percentage in the <2 range: 0.1 percent

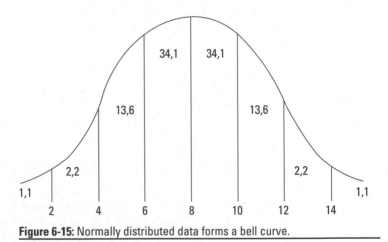

**Figure 6-15:** Normally distributed data forms a bell curve.

# Making inferences and justifying conclusions

Students discover statistics as a way to find out about a population or group without necessarily gathering information from every person in that population. This includes making *inferences* — conclusions based on evidence. When looking at methods for making determinations about populations of events using statistical methods, students discuss whether the methods are reliable — for example, whether the people polled are actually representative of the entire population.

Students also explore uses of *randomization* to improve the accuracy of data. For example, in clinical trials of new medications, participants in the study are almost always chosen randomly for the two groups — the group that receives the medication and the other group that gets the placebo, for example. This approach lessens the chance that some other factor will skew the results. For example, if one group consisted exclusively of men and the other of women, results could be influenced by the sex of the participants rather than by whether the medication was more effective than the placebo.

With your child, examine a recent poll conducted on a political issue. Discuss all of the components used in gathering data, such as the size of the sample population, the means of gathering data, and the interpretation of the results. Share your opinions on the reliability of the conclusions drawn from the data.

Identify instances when randomizing data collection is appropriate for statistical validity and to remove the potential for bias (in other words, to ensure that the data isn't slanted in any particular direction).

## Exploring conditional probability and probability rules

High-school math includes the study of conditional probability — that is, the likelihood that the outcome of one event will influence the outcome of another event. Students explore techniques for determining whether two events are *independent* (neither event influences the other event) or *conditional* (the probability of one event occurring is influenced by whether the other event occurs).

Students also discover how to use data to predict the likelihood of certain events when multiple options are involved. The probability of compound events (when the same trial is attempted multiple times with the same circumstances) is also addressed in these standards.

Here's a sample problem: You randomly draw two cards from a standard deck of 52 playing cards. What are your odds of drawing two clubs?

A deck of cards has 13 clubs, meaning you have a 13 in 52 or 1 in 4 chance of drawing a club as the first card. For the second draw, only 12 clubs remain out of 51 total cards. This results in a 4 out of 17 chance that you'll pull a club on the second draw. To determine the probability of this occurring in consecutive draws, multiply the two ratios:

$$\frac{1}{\cancel{4}} \times \frac{\cancel{4}}{17} = \frac{1}{17}$$

You have a 1 in 17 chance of drawing two clubs consecutively. Feeling lucky?

Play card games in which keeping track of which cards have been played gives you an advantage, such as blackjack, pinochle, spades, and hearts. Count cards (keep track of how many aces have been played, for example) and discuss the likelihood that the next card you receive or that someone plays will be a certain card. To make this activity more challenging, do the math.

## *Using probability to make decisions*

One of the most compelling reasons to develop a knack for calculating probabilities is because this skill often enables you to make better decisions. Students use probability to assess the likelihood of the number of occurrences or events within a set of data and then use that information to answer questions or draw conclusions based on the results. Students also make use of probability to determine the outcome of events based on chance and to analyze decision-making in certain scenarios.

# Chapter 7

# Helping Your Child Achieve English Language Arts Standards in K–5

• • • • • • • • • • • • • • • • • • • • • • • • • • • • • • • • • • • • • •

### In This Chapter

▶ Reviewing the anchor standards

▶ Establishing foundational skills

▶ Leaping into literature

▶ Understanding informational texts

▶ Speaking, listening, and grasping the rules of language

• • • • • • • • • • • • • • • • • • • • • • • • • • • • • • • • • • • • • •

*T*he ability to read, write, and discuss literature and informational texts is critical to your child's success in school, regardless of the grade or subject. After all, one of the only things common to all subject areas is the need to read, write, and carry on informed conversations about content. Because these skills are so central to the rest of school and life, you want to do everything you can to support your child's abilities in these areas.

The Common Core Standards for English language arts outline expectations for reading, writing, speaking and listening, and the conventions of language for kindergarten through Grade 12. The standards are divided by specific aspects of English language arts and by grade, so you can keep a close eye on how well your child is progressing during each school year.

I point out some of the important concepts addressed at each grade level, but for a comprehensive look at the standards visit www.corestandards.org. Before diving into the standards, it's worth noting that your child's literacy skills are significantly impacted by the example you set as a parent. Although you may not think about it, the type and number of words your child hears spoken before she can read impacts her ability to acquire basic literacy skills. Basically, you are your child's first reading teacher, and the lessons she learns from you impact her for the rest of her life.

# Looking at the Anchor Standards

The anchor standards are a great place to start when getting familiar with the Common Core Standards for English language arts. The anchor standards, formally called the College and Career Readiness Anchor Standards, indicate a "finish line" of sorts. They aren't specific to any grade level, but they do indicate the skills that a student should have in reading, writing, speaking and listening, and language by the time she graduates from high school. By taking a look at where your student is headed with the anchor standards, you'll be better able to understand the grade-by-grade requirements and why they are important.

You can use the anchor standards regardless of what grade your child is in. A good way to think about them is to determine the skills your child currently has (based on schoolwork and your own observations), compare that to the expectations of the grade she is in, and then look at the big picture to see how far she has to go to meet the anchor standard in a given area.

## Reading

The ten anchor standards for reading give you a clear picture of the reading skills needed for college and career. The major components include:

- **Determining and using key ideas and details:** The first three anchor standards are grouped under this heading. After mastering all of the standards in this strand, your child should be able to read a text and make inferences, draw conclusions, and cite evidence to support these thoughts. For example, your child can use clues in the text to figure out something that is not specifically stated, and she can cite events in a story that support conclusions she draws from the text. She should also be able to read and determine the main ideas or themes using specific details from what she has read. Finally, your child looks at how specific individuals or actions develop or unfold during the course of the plot or timeline in what she is reading.

✔ **Analyzing craft and structure:** These three anchor standards involve diving into the nuts and bolts of what is being read. Students look at specific vocabulary used; the overall structure of a text, including why certain information is given at certain times; and the point of view of the author or the overall perspective of the writing.

# Simplifying the issue of text complexity

As you read through the Common Core Standards for English language arts, you see that the topic of text complexity is frequently referenced. This is because of the emphasis placed on ensuring that students are reading texts of appropriate complexity at each grade level. When you hear someone say that a student is reading "on grade level," it means that the child can proficiently read texts that are of appropriate quantitative or qualitative complexity for her current grade. Here's how quantitative and qualitative complexity are determined:

✔ **Quantitative** text complexity is typically measured by how long sentences are and the types of words used. Generally speaking, a computer can measure the quantitative complexity of a text and generate a score that indicates

which grade levels are appropriate. The Common Core Standards use Lexile scores to determine the quantitative complexity of a text. The ranges for the appropriate Lexile scores for each grade can be found in Appendix A of the English language arts standards.

✔ **Qualitative** text complexity sometimes reveals information that a computerized quantitative measurement can't. For example, if a text is written in simple language but uses many words, phrases, and expressions that are unfamiliar to students, it is more complex.

Students who enter a grade reading far above or below grade level need additional support to encourage or sustain growth in their reading abilities.

✔ **Pulling together knowledge and ideas:** The three anchor standards under this heading involve using information gathered from multiple sources, making determinations about the reasoning and/or argumentation used by authors, and comparing how multiple texts address a similar topic.

✔ **Considering the range and complexity of texts:** This standard rounds out the anchor standards for reading and addresses the need for students to successfully comprehend literature and informational texts as they read independently. This standard relies more on the successful completion of the previous nine anchor standards rather than introducing new skills.

# Writing

The ten anchor standards for writing outline the types of writing students will complete, along with specific skills related to writing and research processes. Similar to the anchor standards for reading, these standards represent the end result of mastering writing skills in kindergarten through Grade 12.

✔ **Writing with different text types and purposes:** The first three anchor standards in writing address argumentative writing (such as an editorial in a newspaper), explanatory writing (text that tells the reader how to do something), and narrative writing (text that tells a story or describes a sequence of events). The standards include components for effectively using each type of writing, including citing specific evidence and details and using text structure and the order in which information is presented.

✔ **Producing and distributing writing:** The three anchor standards under this heading are related to the writing process, including developing writing that is geared toward an appropriate audience, using revisions and edits to strengthen writing, and effectively using technology to make writing more accessible to a broader audience.

✔ **Researching to build and present knowledge:** These three anchor standards focus on the research process, including the evaluation of sources and the selection of evidence to support a conclusion or argument.

✓ **Evaluating the range of writing:** Similar to the final anchor standard for reading, this standard is summative in nature. It states that students should be able to write within various time frames (either within short amounts of time or over longer periods when doing research and making significant revisions), for various reasons, and for different audiences.

Appendix C of the English language arts standards has samples of student writing that you and your child can review. This will help both of you get a better grasp on the writing skills required by the standards.

## Speaking and listening

The anchor standards for speaking and listening center around the idea that college- and career-ready students must be able to effectively work in collaboration with others and to present information to audiences in various formats. Just like the reading and writing standards, these anchor standards are the result of skills developed from kindergarten through Grade 12.

✓ **Increasing comprehension and collaboration:** The three standards in this section outline skills that require students to work with partners to develop, present, and receive information. This includes the ability to use various forms of mediums in presentations and to examine a person's point of view and assess evidence and other information.

✓ **Presenting knowledge and ideas:** These three standards focus on students' abilities to present for various purposes and in front of audiences, using mediums and representations of data to make presentations more effective.

## Language

The anchor standards for language focus on mastery of the standard rules and conventions of the English language, stylistic uses of language, and skills relating to the acquisition and use of vocabulary.

✔ **Grasping the conventions of standard English:** The two standards under this heading indicate the need for mastery and proper use of grammar and writing skills. The grade-level standards give more specific guidance on exactly what students should know.

✔ **Using knowledge of language:** The one standard in this section deals primarily with how the use of language differs depending on the circumstances. Students learn to make stylistic choices for different audiences and writing purposes.

✔ **Monitoring vocabulary acquisition and use:** The three anchor standards in this section focus on using vocabulary appropriately and determining its meaning. Some standards refer to vocabulary words used in conversations and in readings that are appropriate for the grade level. For more specific guidance on vocabulary usage and potential difficult words that may be encountered, contact your child's teacher for guidance.

# Mastering Foundational Reading Skills

Students use the standards for foundational skills in kindergarten through Grade 5. These standards are the first stepping stones toward literacy skills that are expanded in later grades. For parents, one of the best things about these standards is that you don't have to be an English major to understand the concepts students are asked to master. However, if you're intimidated by the prospect of unpacking skills and concepts related to teaching reading, I outline the basics of what your child needs to know.

Don't forget to check out the resources available in Appendix A of the English language arts standards. Within, you'll find even more specific guidance on the skills and concepts your child needs to master.

## Kindergarten

In kindergarten, students get familiar with the appearance of printed text and how words are organized on a page, such as spacing and uppercase and lowercase letters. They also make the connection that words they hear spoken can be put into text form. Students also use words that rhyme and are able to break down words into syllables and phonemes. *Phonemes* are the smallest units of sound that distinguish one word from another word with different meaning, such as the letter *c* in the word *cat.*

Finally, students practice phonics and begin to read words that appear frequently in texts for beginning readers.

# Grade 1

Students extend their understanding of specific features in printed text, such as capitalizing the first letter of the first word and adding punctuation to the end of sentences. They also explore phonemes at a deeper level, learning to sound out single-syllable words into separate phonemes. For example, with the word *cat,* this involves sounding out each letter into distinct parts. Students continue to use phonics to read one- and two-syllable words, including words that end in *–e* and words with inflectional endings. *Inflectional endings* are suffixes that change a word from singular to plural, such as *dog* to *dogs,* or change the tense of a word, such as *rain* to *rained.* They continue to read appropriately leveled texts with fluency and accuracy, which means they read without a lot of stopping and starting and say and understand words correctly.

# Grade 2

In Grade 2, students continue to work with phonics, including the use of short and long vowel sounds. They continue to use their understanding of phonemes, syllables, and vowel sounds to decode words. Students in Grade 2 should also correctly spell commonly misspelled words appropriate to their grade level. Students are expected to continue reading grade-level texts independently and orally and to use context clues to support their understanding of what they've read. It's important to emphasize to your child that it's 100 percent acceptable to reread a text in order to understand it better.

# Grade 3

Students work to read and understand multisyllable words, along with common prefixes (such as un- and re-) and derivational suffixes. *Derivational suffixes* are endings added to words that give the words new meaning, but that are still derived from the original meaning — for example, changing *run* to *runner, music* to *musician,* or *help* to *helpful.* Students also learn to use and spell words with Latin suffixes, such as sup-*port,* de-*pend,* and pro-*gress.*

Don't get confused trying to categorize different types of prefixes and suffixes. It's more important that your child can recognize a prefix and suffix when it's used, understand how it affects the meaning of the root word, and read and comprehend the word when she sees it in a text.

Students in Grade 3 continue to read grade-level texts, including prose and poetry, fluently and keep using context clues to find meaning when something is unclear.

# Grades 4–5

In Grades 4–5, students use what they have learned about the relationships between letter combinations and sounds to decode and find the meaning of words with multiple syllables. As in other grades, the standards seek to ensure that students continue to read texts that are at grade level. It's important that you closely monitor your child's reading comprehension and make sure she stays on track. In these grades, learning to read has largely given way to reading to learn, so the standards focus on the application of decoding strategies as students read various texts.

# Reading and Understanding Literature

The reading standards for literature give a clear picture of skills and concepts that are essential to the development of your child's reading abilities on a year-to-year basis. These standards are used when your child reads fictional literature, which according to the Common Core Standards constitutes a majority of her reading material until Grade 4. At that point, the standards indicate that students should be reading 50 percent fictional literature and 50 percent informational texts (or literary nonfiction).

Be sure to consult the resources available in Appendixes A and B of the English language arts standards. Appendix A contains further descriptions and explanations of the reading expectations, while Appendix B identifies texts that are of appropriate complexity for specific grade levels.

The standards for reading literature align directly with the anchor standards for reading and also use the same subheadings:

- Key ideas and details
- Craft and structure
- Integration of knowledge and ideas
- Range of reading and level of text complexity

Because these subheadings are repeated in each grade, you can easily compare the demands of the standards in your child's current grade with future grades and with the college- and career-ready skills described in the anchor standards.

Anchor standard eight isn't used when reading literature. Because this standard focuses on claims and supporting evidence in text, the grade-by-grade progressions for standard eight are limited to the informational text standards.

## Kindergarten

In kindergarten, students answer questions — with support — about specific details from a text that has been read to them, along with being able to retell aspects of the story and identify characters. They also practice naming the author and illustrator and understanding the job of each. Students pay attention to illustrations and practice describing how illustrations or pictures are related to the story. After reading more than one story, students are expected to describe how stories are similar or different based on the events that take place in the lives of the characters. A major emphasis is placed on participating in group reading and listening activities.

# Grade 1

Students continue to focus on detailed information gained from a text while also showing that they understand the main ideas conveyed in what they read. They are asked to consider more detail in their understanding of characters and significant happenings in stories. Students explore characteristics relating to the structure of written materials by pointing out words that evoke certain sensory responses, distinguishing the differences among texts, and recognizing the person whose voice is active within a text. They continue to use pictures and illustrations to find out more about what they're reading.

# Grade 2

Students begin to interact with texts by asking questions such as *who, what, when, where, why,* and *how* in order to analyze what they are reading. They are able to remember stories that they read and identify the main ideas, along with providing details on the actions of characters within the story. When reading a story, students recognize the structure of a plot and know that the beginning starts the story and the ending provides a conclusion. Within a story, students understand that characters have different perspectives and can represent them by using alternate voices. In their reading, students examine more than one version of a story written by a different author or from another culture.

# Grade 3

In Grade 3, students use specific textual evidence to gain information pertaining to what they've read, and can explain how a main idea is communicated within a story. When reading, students can identify how characters affect the unfolding of events. Use of vocabulary grows more complex as students encounter words with literal and nonliteral meanings, causing them to draw upon their skills of inference to discern the accurate meaning of certain terms. Students learn to refer to specific parts of texts, such as a chapter in a book or a scene in a play. As they become more adept at reading to gather insights, students show that they can separate their own selves from the text and recognize that their point of view (with regard to the unfolding of action) is different from that of the characters in the story. Students analyze in increased detail the contribution of illustrations to the meaning of texts. The ability to determine the central ideas of a work of literature expands, and students are asked to analyze the messages conveyed by the same author in multiple books, such as books in a series.

# Grade 4

In Grade 4, students infer information, summarize, and make use of details to develop a greater understanding of aspects of literature such as characters and events. They continue to use context clues to determine the meanings of words and allusions to other works of literature, such as Greek mythology. Students dive into the structure of poems and distinguish specific aspects such as verse and meter; they also identify components of plays and other dramatic texts, including the characters and technical descriptions such as stage directions. When reading, students distinguish between writings in first and third person. *First person* refers to writing in which the narrator uses pronouns like *I* and *me*. In essence, the narrator acknowledges her own voice and speaks from her perspective. *Third person* is used when characters in a text are referred to as *he, she, him, her,* and so on. Third person is a more formal style of writing that detaches the narrator from the action taking place and describes it from an outside point of view.

# Grade 5

In Grade 5, students use quotes from their reading to support statements made regarding the meaning of a text. They also identify the theme presented in a work of literature and examine the reactions of characters to difficult situations within the plot of a story. Students are asked to analyze multiple characters and their connections and relationships.

Students identify and understand figurative language, which describes something by comparing it to something else. This includes distinguishing between similes, which use the words *like* or *as,* and metaphors.

- ✔ **Simile:** The students ran down the hallway as fast as racehorses.

- ✔ **Metaphor:** The students agreed that math class lasted a lifetime.

When reading, students identify how the point of view can influence the meaning of a text and continue to examine the impact of illustrations on perceptions of writing. They also investigate how a specific theme is addressed in multiple pieces of literature.

Because the end of Grade 5 is a significant milestone, you want to make sure your child is reading texts of appropriate complexity by the time she reaches the end of Grade 5.

# Reading and Deciphering Informational Texts

You'll notice many similarities between the reading standards for literature and the reading standards for informational texts, but it's important to remember that the standards for informational texts are used with nonfiction materials. Your child may easily grasp these skills and concepts when reading fictional literature, but informational texts are often more complex, and students sometimes perceive them to be less interesting because there isn't a "story" involved. With that in mind, take a look at some of the major skills and concepts in kindergarten through Grade 5.

## Kindergarten

With adult support, kindergarten students use details from a text to successfully answer questions, ask questions of others, pinpoint the central idea(s), and identify any relationships that exist between parts of a text. They also identify unfamiliar words and attempt to understand their meaning. When looking at a book, students are able to distinguish the parts of a book, such as the covers and internal parts of a book, along with identifying the author and/or illustrator and their contributions to the text. Because students read informational texts to gain information on specific topics, they begin the process of identifying information that supports the author's purpose for writing. Just as they were asked to do with literature, students compare how the same subject is addressed by different texts.

# Grade 1

Students in Grade 1 continue to focus on key details and relationships between specific aspects of a text, such as how two events may be related. They also find the meanings of unfamiliar words and use specific aspects of the text, such as the table of contents, appendix, and glossary, to gather information. Students are asked to tell the difference between what is written in the text and what is represented in illustrations. They continue to use specific details to explain how ideas are supported, along with comparing and contrasting multiple texts about similar subject matter. In Grade 1, students begin to read nonfiction texts independently at times, so be sure to monitor your child's understanding of the material she is reading. Transitioning from reading fiction to nonfiction can be challenging for some students, so monitor understanding of these texts by asking questions about individuals or events mentioned in the reading.

# Grade 2

Just as students do with literature in Grade 2, they use the questions *who, what, when, where, why,* and *how* to gain specific information from a text. This allows them to find the central idea(s) of a text with several paragraphs. As they read, students explain the relationships between various ideas, events, and other aspects presented in a text, and they are able to use headings, menus, and other parts of a text to identify important information. Because students encounter a variety of words that are specific to certain subjects, such as science or social studies, take the time to ensure that they understand the vocabulary used when referring to specific content. In some instances, students determine the purpose that an author had for writing a specific text and analyze the main ideas and arguments outlined in more than one text.

# Grade 3

In Grade 3, students continue to cite textual evidence when answering questions, including how details contribute to understanding the central idea(s) and theme(s) in a text. They also continue to examine the relationships between events in a text, with a specific emphasis on the order of events and/or cause-and-effect relationships. As they read, students expand beyond the text to include Internet-based resources, such as search engines and other online material related to the text they are reading, and they continue to use illustrations and other graphics to understand information presented in a text. Students show that they understand why sentences in a paragraph are in a certain order, and how each sentence is related to the next.

# Grade 4

Students in Grade 4 continue to refer to specific textual evidence when summarizing or inferring information. They also identify central idea(s) based on specific information from the text, along with accurately summarizing information presented in a text. When reading, students are expected to identify why things occur, or need to occur, in a certain order based on their understanding of what they've read. Students explain how information is organized, as it relates to the development of concepts, in a text. For example, in a social-studies class, students may be asked to recognize that text is written along a chronological timeline. With some texts, students analyze similarities and differences between first-hand and secondhand accounts, which lays the foundation for evaluating the legitimacy of sources in later grades. Students continue to examine information presented in various forms, whether in print or with a graphical representation, in order to expand their understanding of a specific topic. They also use information gathered from more than one text on a similar topic, and can write or speak using that information.

# Grade 5

In Grade 5, students use specific quotes to demonstrate and support their understanding of a text. They also identify at least two central ideas in a text and find information in a text that supports those ideas, along with accurately summarizing what they've read. Students are asked to describe the connections and relationships among multiple aspects of a text. For example, students may be asked to explain why two historical events are related. Students compare the organization of information and how topics are presented in more than one text, along with being able to successfully navigate sources to find a specific piece of needed information. Doing so allows them to show how evidence supports specific ideas and to use evidence from multiple sources.

# Writing Clearly and Effectively

The writing standards emphasize more than just putting together a five-paragraph essay. Starting in the early grades, the writing standards emphasize writing to inform, argue specific points, and narrate stories and events. Students learn to use various sources and write with accountability to the sources used in order to strengthen their writing. The foundation established by the writing standards in kindergarten through Grade 5 is an essential building block toward developing student readers and writers that are college and career ready by the time they graduate from high school. As with the reading standards, the writing standards in each grade level follow the breakdown of the anchor standards I address earlier in this chapter.

Refer to Appendixes A, B, and C of the English language arts standards for more resources on the types of writing addressed in the Common Core Standards. Appendix A provides descriptions of the types of writing, Appendix B contains samples of appropriately complex reading material, and Appendix C includes samples of student writing from different grade levels.

## Kindergarten

Students draw, speak, and write to communicate their opinions, to inform a reader about a specific subject, or to communicate about a series of events. This represents their introduction to writing for the purpose of persuasion, argumentation, and narration. Students then learn to take feedback in order to strengthen what they have written, along with using technology (such as word processors, publishing programs, and the Internet) to enhance their finished product. Students also practice their skills in research by working independently and with partners to gather information about a specific topic from relevant sources. The major outcomes of the writing standards in kindergarten are focused on learning the essential processes that support effective writing, rather than on the end product of a written text. The emphasis on producing a finished writing product begins in Grade 3.

# Grade 1

Students continue to write to express their opinions, inform readers about a specific topic, and produce a narrative. However, students also focus on additional details, such as providing supporting statements and evidence to enhance their writing, along with using words that signify the order of events and closure. Students also continue to strengthen their writing by integrating feedback from their teacher and other students, and they produce digital forms of writing by working independently and with their peers in class. Students continue to practice researching and writing with a focus on gathering information from appropriate sources.

# Grade 2

In Grade 2, the writing process extends to include adding introductory remarks that provide an effective beginning. This applies to writing that is done for the purposes of providing an opinion, explaining information, and describing a narrative. Writing also becomes more detailed through the use of supporting statements, facts, and evidence from sources and experiences. The emphasis in Grade 2 is on developing the structure of writing so that the overall organization and the details within more effectively communicate the student's purpose for writing. Students continue to revise writing, use digital resources, and work with others to conduct research in which they consult numerous sources on a specific topic and/ or gather their own data if they are reporting on a scientific experiment.

# Grade 3

In Grade 3, students begin to engage in the writing process, with the end result being a finished written product. As such, the standards in this grade are divided to provide more detail. Each type of writing (argument, information/explanation, and narrative) has specific guidelines for introducing the topic; supporting it with evidence and details; making specific word choices, including linking words; and developing an effective conclusion. Students continue to revise and enhance their writing, focusing on the processes of pre-writing and editing, along with practicing keyboarding in their use of technology.

The use of research progresses into completing research projects focused on specific topics. Evidence used to support conclusions in their research is collected and organized into categories. In Grade 3, students write in a more routine manner, with emphasis on the various aspects of the writing process and in order to write on various topics for different purposes.

# Grade 4

In Grade 4, students use increasingly detailed steps in the writing process. For example, students not only use details to support their writing but also organize their writing to present related points together, thereby strengthening their ability to persuade or make an argument. Students also employ linking phrases, such as *for example,* to connect their thoughts with supporting evidence. The increased use of details is also applied to the concluding section of writing, which is another way to convey convincing information. Editing in Grade 4 incorporates more detail, including an increased focus on appropriate usage of the rules of style and grammar (see "Grasping English Language Rules and Conventions" later in this chapter or refer to the language standards at www.corestandards.org).

The expectations for typing skills become more specific in Grade 4, as the writing standards indicate that students should be able to type at least one page in a "sitting." Although the standards don't give a specific time frame, I assume this means a reasonable amount of time that students may have in class to type their writing. In Grade 4, students begin to connect the outcomes of the reading standards with the expectations of the writing standards. This includes using specific textual evidence, inferences and conclusions drawn from reading, and other information gathered from consulting multiple sources. Students use these skills and this information to produce writing of various lengths on given topics.

# Grade 5

The writing standards in Grade 5 build on the many skills introduced in Grade 4, while continuing to add emphasis on providing supporting details and using writing conventions.

The use of clauses is introduced to give students a tool to connect their opinions with evidence, and that evidence with a specific outcome in their writing. Editing and revising to strengthen writing continues in Grade 5, along with increased expectations for student use of technology. Students are expected to type at least two pages (versus one page in Grade 4) in a "sitting," which suggests that a considerable amount of a student's writing should be done on a computer so that she can practice becoming more efficient with keystrokes. Students also expand their research skills by applying the expectations of the Grade 5 reading standards to the information pulled from sources consulted in their writing, resulting in more detailed evidence to support topics and deeper analysis of the purpose(s) of authors consulted in their research.

# Speaking and Listening Standards

The aim of the speaking and listening standards is to assist students in learning to communicate effectively in a group setting. Many times during a student's academic career, she'll need to be able to work with a group to accomplish certain outcomes. This may mean having a conversation about something she's read in class or completing a formal project that is a major part of the grade for a certain subject. Either way, the skills associated with effectively sharing information and actively listening are essential to working well with others. After all, isn't that a major part of daily life as an adult?

## Kindergarten

In kindergarten, students practice the art of conversation in groups, with a specific emphasis on following established norms like taking turns and being quiet while others are sharing information. However, the emphasis isn't on passive listening. Rather, students practice asking questions of the speaker to make sure they understand the information being presented. When it's their turn to talk, students are expected to speak clearly and in detail about topics that are appropriate to kindergarten, using illustrations or other representations as supports.

# Grade 1

Skills in speaking and listening extend in Grade 1 to include more complex forms of discussion. Not only do students speak and ask questions about what they are learning in class, but they also begin to use comments made by others in their own remarks as a demonstration of their ability to actively listen to contributions made by other speakers. This may include agreeing or disagreeing with a statement made by someone else and providing further information on the topic as it was presented in class or through a reading. Students present information with detail, sometimes aided by visual supports, by speaking in complete sentences.

# Grade 2

The expectations for participating in group discussions are more complex in Grade 2. While still following norms established by the group, students gain the attention of the group in order to speak without talking over one another. Students continue to use comments made by other students in their own remarks, but they also connect statements made by one student to something said by another student. With the addition of this skill, students learn to incorporate more and more of the group's discussion into their thought processes. Students also continue to seek information through conversation that furthers their comprehension of the topic at hand. In presentations of information, students continue to develop their speaking skills by using complete sentences that include details related to the topic at hand. Along with the use of visual aids introduced in earlier grades, students make use of technology to record readings of texts used in class. Because this can be an intimidating task for students, you'll want to practice doing this at home if you have a computer, smartphone, or other device with voice-recording capabilities.

# Grade 3

The speaking and listening standards advance significantly in difficulty in Grade 3. Apart from participating effectively in various forms of discussion, whether with one other student, with multiple students, or in a group conversation with the teacher, students must also prepare to participate.

This includes reading related texts in advance so that they can contribute to the conversation with evidence from their readings. Students also prepare to provide a detailed explanation of their remarks and how they contribute to the larger discussion of the group. As with the reading skills, students pinpoint the central idea(s) of material that is presented. Presentation skills in Grade 3 expand to consider the rate at which a student speaks, aiming to make students aware whether they are speaking too quickly or too slowly. This is a factor during student presentations and with any recordings students make of reading or presenting information. Proper conventions of language for Grade 3 are also considered; I cover those in the next section of this chapter.

## Grade 4

The expectations for speaking and listening continue to increase in Grade 4 as students participate in more and more elaborate and detailed conversations. Students reference materials they've read beforehand and use specific details in their statements. Using their understanding of the topic at hand, students ask questions of other students, refer to comments made by others, and make their own statements that add to the overall discussion. Grade 4 introduces the skill of paraphrasing information that was read or shared by someone else. In activities that require a group to work collaboratively, students must accomplish individual assignments that contribute to the success of the group as assigned by the teacher. Student presentations are organized appropriately for the topic and filled with detailed information that contributes to the main purpose of the report. The use of visual aids, voice recordings, and other presentation aids continues in Grade 4. A new expectation for student presentations is the ability to determine when they should speak formally (such as during a presentation to a large group) and when informal speech is appropriate (such as in conversation with one or several peers).

## Grade 5

Many of the skills introduced in Grade 4 are built upon in Grade 5, including making use of information gathered from reading and listening to others speak. Students continue to demonstrate their ability to ask questions that are specifically related to the comments of others, along with identifying the main points of a conversation and/or text through summarizing information. Student presentations continue to show the ability to organize information into an appropriate and understandable format, with the integration of visual and audio components when applicable. The use of proper speech and language continues based on the nature of the presentation and the audience.

# English Language Rules and Conventions

The standards for language outline the grade levels at which students should master particular aspects of the English language used in reading, writing, speaking, and listening. Instead of listing every rule, convention, and practice covered in the language standards, I provide a brief overview that captures the essence of each grade level. For a comprehensive look at the language standards, visit www.corestandards.org. It's important to remember that these skills and concepts aren't taught or learned in isolation. They are meant to help students communicate better as speakers and writers and to increase reading comprehension.

## Kindergarten

Students in kindergarten are getting familiar with sounds, letters, and the meanings of words, and the language standards support the development of these understandings. Capitalization, punctuation at the beginning and end of sentences, and the use of phonics to aid spelling all play key parts in the kindergarten standards. Here are a few of the other topics covered:

- Nouns and verbs
- Interrogatives (words used to ask questions, such as *what* and *why*)
- Plural nouns
- Prepositions (words that indicate the position or relationship of one thing to another)

✔ Antonyms (words with opposite meanings)

✔ The difference between words with more than one meaning (*bat*, for example) and verbs with slightly different but related meanings (such as *look* and *search*)

✔ The use of affixes (prefixes and suffixes that change the meaning of a word)

# Grade 1

In Grade 1, students tackle uppercase and lowercase letters, different types of pronouns, and common adjectives. They also use sentences with various types of ending punctuation (periods, question marks, and exclamation marks). Students broaden their understanding of vocabulary by using context clues, affixes, and root words to discover the meanings of unknown words. Some of the other skills and concepts addressed in Grade 1 are:

✔ Understanding basic subject-verb agreement

✔ Using verbs of different tenses (past, present, and future)

✔ Working with conjunctions (words that join sentences, such as *and* and *or*)

✔ Using commas to separate items in a series

✔ Separating words into different groups based on various criteria (such as size or function)

✔ Distinguishing between similar adjectives (such as *damp* and *soaked*)

✔ Making connections between vocabulary words and things to which they can be related in the real world

# Grade 2

Students work with more specialized forms of nouns, pronouns, and other parts of speech in Grade 2. They learn to capitalize proper nouns and to add punctuation within a sentence, such as apostrophes in contractions. Students continue to use their understanding of context clues and root words to identify the meanings of unknown words and compound words. Here's a sampling of the other topics covered by the standards in Grade 2:

✔ Irregular forms of plural nouns (such as *deer* and *geese*)

✔ Reflexive pronouns (pronouns such as *himself* or *yourself*, usually used when the subject and object of a sentence are the same — for example, "He likes *himself*.")

✔ Past tense of irregular verbs (such as *spoke* and *sang*)

✔ Commas used in salutations in letters

✔ The use of print and electronic reference books (such as a dictionary or encyclopedia)

# Grade 3

In Grade 3, students are able to explain the parts of speech (nouns, verbs, adjectives, pronouns, and adverbs) and how they are used in sentences. They also extend their use of punctuation to include using possessives, writing addresses, and appropriately using commas and quotation marks when explicitly citing verbal statements. Along with the continued use of context clues to determine the meanings of unfamiliar words, students expand their use of figurative language. Some other topics addressed in Grade 3 are:

✔ Making sure a pronoun in a sentence agrees with its *antecedent* (the preceding noun). For example, in the following sentence, *Bob* and *his* are in agreement based on gender and number: *Bob* threw away *his* old baseball glove.

✔ Using comparative and superlative adjectives and adverbs. A comparative adjective involves comparing two nouns, such as saying that someone is *taller* than someone else. A superlative adjective involves comparing something to the rest of a group, such as observing that someone is the *tallest* in her family. Comparative and superlative adverbs operate in the same way with adverbs — for example, saying that someone arrived *earlier* (comparative) or *earliest* (superlative).

✔ Figuring out coordinating and subordinating conjunctions. Coordinating conjunctions connect two clauses that are unrelated using words such as *but, and,* and *or.* Subordinating conjunctions connect two clauses that are related in some way using words like *because, as,* and *that.*

 ✔ Using prefixes and suffixes to form additional words.

 ✔ Differentiating between words related to the likelihood of an event (such as *probably* and *certainly*) and a state of mind (such as *knowing* and *assuming*).

# Grade 4

Students in Grade 4 continue to use various parts of speech and punctuation in more specialized instances, along with editing their own work to ensure proper use and complete sentences. Vocabulary usage grows more extensive as students use additional affixes and figurative language. A few of the skills and concepts identified by the standards in Grade 4 include:

 ✔ Relative pronouns (such as *who* and *whom*) and relative adverbs (such as *when* and *where*)

 ✔ Past, present, and future progressive verb tenses (such as *he was eating, he is eating,* and *he will be eating*)

 ✔ Words that are often confused with other similar words (such as *to, too,* and *two*)

 ✔ Use of the suffix –*graph* to determine the meaning of words

 ✔ The meaning of similes (comparisons that use *like* or *as*) and metaphors

 ✔ Synonyms and antonyms

# Grade 5

In Grade 5, students use more parts of speech, punctuation, and types of words and phrases. This includes writing and speaking in various tenses and making use of different types of punctuation to accentuate text for various purposes. Students continue to use context clues to discern the meanings of unknown words, words with more than one meaning, and unfamiliar or new expressions. Here's a look at some of the important topics in Grade 5:

- ✔ Conjunctions (words that connect sentence parts, such as *and* or *but*) and interjections (exclamatory words that add feelings to a sentence, such as *Oh* or *Ouch*).

- ✔ The perfect verb tense — a verb tense that indicates an action being completed, such as "I *have danced* today, I *had danced* before, and I *will have danced* three times by the end of the month."

- ✔ Correlative conjunctions — pairs of words that combine parts of a sentence, such as *neither* and *nor* in the statement, "*Neither* Jacob *nor* Justin wanted to come inside."

- ✔ Commas in a series and with introductory clauses.

- ✔ The meaning of common sayings — for example, "The early bird gets the worm."

- ✔ Similes, metaphors, and *homographs* (words that are spelled the same but have different meanings, such as *bat* and *rose*).

## Keeping up with Standard 10

Standard 10 functions as a filter through which all the standards should be read in order to ensure that students are progressing appropriately in reading and writing materials that are of appropriate complexity for a particular grade. Earlier in this chapter, I discuss the use of text complexity as a means of determining appropriate texts for each grade level. A second consideration is the range and quality of materials the students read. The standards give specific guidance on the types of texts that should be read at certain intervals.

- ✔ **By Grade 4** students should read 50 percent literature and 50 percent informational texts (including literary nonfiction).

- ✔ **By Grade 8** students should read 45 percent literature and 55 percent informational texts (including literary nonfiction).

- ✔ **By Grade 12** students should read 30 percent literature and 70 percent informational texts (including literary nonfiction).

The percentages for each grade benchmark refer to the entire scope of texts that students read across the curriculum, including the informational texts they read in content areas like science and social studies. They aren't meant to define expectations for English or reading classes alone.

# Chapter 8

# Raising the Bar: English Language Arts Standards in Grades 6–12

· · · · · · · · · · · · · · · · · · · · · · · · · · · · · · · · · · · · ·

### In This Chapter

▶ Reading up on literature and informational texts

▶ Stepping up to higher levels of writing

▶ Progressing with speaking and listening skills

▶ Adding more rules of language

· · · · · · · · · · · · · · · · · · · · · · · · · · · · · · · · · · · · ·

*T*he English language arts standards in Grades 6–12 build on the foundation of skills and concepts established in kindergarten through Grade 5. The rigor of these standards escalates quickly, so you'll definitely want to make sure you keep up with all of the changes.

The standards for Grades 6, 7, and 8 reflect the structure of the standards in lower grades. Each grade level is organized separately for reading, writing, speaking and listening, and language standards. However, the organization of the standards changes as students move to higher grade levels.

The standards in high school are grouped into a single set for Grades 9–10 and another set for Grades 11–12. The specific applications of the high-school standards rely on the content covered in your child's classes, so it's important to keep up with his classes and the standards being taught at any given time. For the complete set of standards for English language arts in Grades 6–12, visit www.corestandards.org.

# Reading More Sophisticated Literature and Informational Texts

As you read through the literature and informational-text standards in Grades 6–12, you notice increased expectations for reading skills and reading materials. Students read an increasing percentage of informational texts as they move to higher grade levels, so don't forget to think about this when selecting texts to practice with at home.

I summarize the reading standards for literature and informational texts together in this chapter, even though they're listed as separate sets of standards with the Common Core Standards. Many of the skills are similar but are used with varying text types. Refer to specific standards in each grade if you're looking for the most detailed information on what your child should be able to do when jumping into literature or when taking a look at informational texts.

In Chapter 7, I provide an overview of the anchor standards and how they can be used. Because these standards outline where students should be by the end of Grade 12, look at how your student is doing, what expectations he faces in his current grade level, and how those two compare to the ultimate expectations of the anchor standards.

## Grade 6

In Grade 6, students focus on citing evidence to back up conclusions, inferences, and ideas formed about the main point(s) communicated by a text. The standards emphasize a degree of fidelity to the text, as students must separate their own opinions from what is explicitly stated in a piece of text regarding the plot, themes, and characters involved. In informational text, this includes relying on the details provided about specific events and individuals.

Students continue to work with complex vocabulary, such as figurative language (similes and metaphors, for example) and words that draw meaning from connotation. Words with *connotative* meanings evoke ideas or feelings beyond their textbook definitions. For example, the word *debt* is generally accompanied by negative feelings and thus can have a negative connotation.

In Grade 6, students also examine other aspects of the structure of texts, including the organizational structure in which details are presented and the development of the narrator's or author's point of view. They also examine the similarities and differences between the experience of reading a text and listening to and/or watching it be read, along with how a theme is presented in different genres of writing. Students also determine whether specific arguments are backed up with sufficient support in informational texts.

The skills in the grade-by-grade progression for anchor standard eight in the reading standards are only used with informational texts, not with literature. Standard eight deals with specific claims, arguments, and evidence presented in texts.

## Grade 7

In Grade 7, students begin citing multiple pieces of textual evidence to support their conclusions based on what is read or inferred from literature or informational texts. They're also expected to identify how an idea evolves within a piece of writing, along with summarizing what they've read without interjecting their own opinion. This underscores the emphasis on textual evidence throughout the reading and writing standards. They also examine how parts of a story (such as characters, setting, and conflict) influence each other.

As they read various forms of literature, students study the use of alliteration in poetry and look into how the organization of a text impacts its meaning. As they become more analytic readers, students recognize similarities and differences between the points of view of various characters in literature, and of various authors when reading informational texts.

When listening to and/or viewing an audio or visual representation of a text, students dissect the impact of certain elements such as sound effects, lighting, and camera angles on the presentation and meaning of the original piece of text. Students find similarities and differences between fictional and historically accurate descriptions of the same time period in literature. When reading informational texts, students examine the method of organizing and presenting information used by different authors who wrote about the same thing.

# Grade 8

In Grade 8, students focus not only on using evidence to support conclusions regarding a text but also on selecting the *best* evidence from a text to back their understanding of what is being communicated. They're also able to recognize how the main themes and ideas in a text are related to other elements of the writing, including key details and descriptions of ideas, and how those details and ideas contribute to the development of the story. Along with understanding the figurative and connotative meanings of words, students dissect *analogies* (which compare or contrast one thing with another to communicate meaning, such as "he's as tall and skinny as a beanstalk") and *allusions* (which reference other well-known works of art or literature, such as "she's a real Grinch around the holidays").

Students take a look at the organization of multiple texts and how it can impact style and influence the information a reader takes away from a text. They also make connections between differing points of view in a piece of literature, which can result in comedy or tension. When reading informational texts, students pay attention to the author's point of view and whether he or she acknowledges any information that may contradict what is being presented. Students are expected to examine the reasonableness of the evidence presented and be able to determine when inconclusive or unrelated information is presented.

Expectations for Grade 8 also include determining how closely a film, movie, or play represents the original literature from which it was drawn. When reading informational texts, students explore the pros and cons of using various types of mediums to communicate about a specific subject. Students examine the use of elements of older stories and literature in modern writings, with an eye toward pointing out how the newer version presents information in a new way. With informational texts, students identify situations where texts present information that disagrees with another source.

# Grades 9–10

In Grades 9–10, students use extensive textual evidence and specific details to describe what they've read, and examine the evolution of the main ideas, the role of complex characters or individuals, and other significant components that contribute to the meaning of a text. Building on the understanding of types of vocabulary learned in previous grades, students look into the effect of word choice on how a text is understood and perceived. They continue to examine the influence of a text's structure on its meaning, along with how a writer uses time, including flashbacks and flash-forwards, to evoke certain emotions.

In their reading, students encounter perspectives from different countries and cultures in world literature. Students also look into how an author's point of view impacts what and how he or she writes about certain topics. They also explore and consider how a specific topic or scene is depicted in different art forms, such as the portrayal of a specific part of the Bible in a drama or of one of William Shakespeare's plays in a painting. When students read informational texts, they place more emphasis on the presentation of information in various formats, such as graphical representations or the use of numbers and statistics. Students also look into how an author uses a specific source in his or her writing. When using more than one informational text, students pay attention to how different texts approach the same or related themes.

## Grades 11–12

The expectations for students' reading abilities in Grades 11–12 include an extension of the citation skills from Grades 9–10. In addition, students critique the clarity of texts. They also identify multiple main ideas and how those ideas emerge throughout a text in order to give a detailed and objective summary. In literature, students continue to examine an author's decisions about character development and other parts of a story. When using informational texts, students spend more time looking into the effects of certain people and events on the outcome of the event or topic being studied.

When reading literature or informational texts, students continue trying to understand the reasons behind the choice of certain words. The standards specifically mention reading the works of William Shakespeare but don't refer to specific writings. The informational-text standards make reference to the writings of James Madison in the Federalist Papers, specifically Federalist No. 10, as an example of a text in which the meaning of an important term (faction, for example) is developed within a text. Students continue to examine the impact of a text's structure on meaning and begin to tackle the use of satire, irony, and other literature styles that require discerning the meaning of a text. When reading informational texts, students look critically at the impact of the language the author chooses and how it contributes to the effectiveness of the message being conveyed.

Students experience multiple versions of a piece of literature and think critically about the presentation of each version as it relates to the original. The standards specify that a play by Shakespeare and a play by an American writer should be used, but the actual plays to be used are left to the discretion of teachers, schools, and districts.

The standards also point out that students should read important writings from the eighteenth though the twentieth centuries and indicate how certain subjects are addressed in more than one piece of literature.

When reading informational texts, students continue to review sources with a critical eye and use evidence from sources, whether in a written, visual, or quantitative form, to find the answer to a specified problem. To support students' abilities to assess the reasoning of important documents in United States history, the standards suggest U.S. Supreme Court opinions, the Federalist Papers, and presidential speeches as examples of documents that make worthy topics. The standards for informational texts in this grade band recommend important historical documents, such as the Declaration of Independence and President Abraham Lincoln's second inaugural address, which should be studied for their inherent historical importance and the use of noteworthy rhetoric.

Don't forget to take a look at the resources available in the appendixes to the English language arts standards. Appendix B has samples of appropriate literature and texts for each grade level. Remember, these aren't selections that students have to read. They are only examples of reading materials that are appropriately complex for each grade level.

# Honing Your Child's Writing Skills

Like the writing standards in earlier grades, the writing standards for Grades 6–12 center around three types of writing: argument, informative/explanatory, and narrative. The standards also include expectations for conducting effective research and collecting appropriate source materials, along with guidelines for the process of revising and rewriting.

Take a look at Appendix C of the English language arts standards for samples of student writing. This gives you a great idea of how to gauge your child's progress while also letting him see the work of other students in his grade.

# Grade 6

Writing in Grade 6 requires students to become more detailed. The standards outline various criteria for effective writing depending upon the purpose the student is trying to achieve. Here are a few of the components:

- ✔ **Argument:** Students focus on selecting evidence that will back up what they are writing, along with identifying and using sources that contribute to their arguments. Students are also expected to write a conclusion that solidifies their argument.

- ✔ **Information and explanation:** The standards emphasize the organization and presentation of information, such as the use of formatting, tables, and visual representations to convey meaning. Topics expand through the use of information from relevant sources, and students end formal writings with a conclusion.

- ✔ **Narrative:** Students write to convey or describe an experience with details about important characters and a series of events that occur in a way that makes sense to a reader. This requires students to transition from one section to another in their writing and use words that communicate the order of events and the results. Students also begin to write texts in which characters speak to each other.

The writing standards for Grade 6 also place emphasis on planning, pre-writing, and editing to make the final piece of writing even more effective. Students make use of various resources to gather information and answer a specific question related to research, assuring that selected sources are appropriate and authoritative. When integrating information from various sources, students write with direct quotes and summaries from sources without plagiarizing. This requires students to cite their sources in a basic bibliography.

## Standard 10: Range of writing

For each grade level, Standard 10 in the writing standards outlines expectations for the frequency and length of writing and research students can do. The actual wording of this standard doesn't change from grade to grade. However, the expectations for this standard change to align with the increasing demands of the other standards in each grade.

The integration of technology as a tool for writing continues, as students use the Internet and other tools to write and make their writing available to others. In Grade 6, expectations for keyboarding proficiency include the ability to produce at least three typed pages. As mentioned in the standards in previous grade levels, typing expectations are defined by what a student can do in a "single sitting." I assume that means a reasonable amount of time that a student may have to type in a class at school.

## Grade 7

In Grade 7, writing becomes even more detailed and requires a greater degree of planning. Along with a continued emphasis on details and the use of sources to provide evidence and supporting statements, significant attention is given to making sure students properly organize their writing for maximum effect. Although this looks different depending on the type of writing the student is doing, the skills in gathering and organizing information are very much related. Here are some of the skills needed for writing in Grade 7:

- ✔ **Argument:** Students continue to incorporate appropriate and legitimate evidence into their writing, along with recognizing different points of view that conflict with their own. Students seek to write with a sense of unity and flow by making sure sentences and paragraphs are organized in a logical manner.

- ✔ **Information and explanation:** In their writing, students practice giving an overview of the information they will present, and continue to focus on organizing content so that it flows logically as they present detailed information.

- ✔ **Narrative:** While continuing to write about experiences and/or a series of events, students incorporate a point of view that contributes to the overall meaning of their writing. The organization of events and transitions from one part to the next continue to be important elements of writing, and students incorporate aspects of reflection into the concluding parts of their writing.

The expectations for students to edit and revise their writing continue in Grade 7. Students also evaluate their own success in accomplishing the original purpose of their writing. The use of technology in research, writing, and disseminating a finished piece of writing continues, but students are also expected to cite their sources and provide a hyperlink if possible (when putting written material in an online format).

Students in Grade 7 continue to use information from sources effectively and appropriately to answer research questions, while also using citations in a specified format. Students are expected to determine additional points of inquiry to study in the future based on the results of their original research.

# Grade 8

Writing in Grade 8 requires a greater degree of precision, particularly with regard to how well students identify supporting details to use in their writing and how they choose to organize information within a written text. More emphasis is also placed on the development of the introductory and concluding parts of writing, which students use even more to outline the most important aspects of their writing and to support their overall purpose. Here's a quick glance at some of the writing expectations for Grade 8:

- ✔ **Argument:** In their writing, students tell the difference between their position and an opposing view. They also find and include important supporting evidence. Students explain the connection between evidence and/ or sources used and the student's position on an issue, along with how available evidence relates to an opposing position. Students write a conclusion that flows from and bolsters the claims in the rest of their writing.

- ✔ **Information and explanation:** Students clearly communicate their topic and are successful in organizing information in a way that makes sense to readers. More emphasis is placed on how successful students are in selecting evidence that best supports their efforts to relate information. As with other grade levels, students finish their writing with a conclusion that effectively reinforces information presented in preceding sections of their writing.

✔ **Narrative:** The emphasis on details and the use of organization to allow events to develop continues for narrative writing in Grade 8. Students continue to use reflection to support the development of key aspects in a piece of writing, while also describing relationships between significant pieces of information they include in their writing.

In Grade 8, students continue to pre-write, organize information for use in writing, and make revisions to their writing that enhance the quality of the final product. They also continue to use technology to make their work accessible to others. As in previous grade levels, students integrate details and evidence from selected sources that are relevant and appropriate for their topic without plagiarizing. As they complete their research, students also identify topics for further study.

In previous grades, the standards specifically outlined expectations for how much a student would be able to type. You won't find these specific expectations in Grade 8 or beyond. The assumption is that students will be proficient typists by the time they reach this grade level.

## Grades 9–10

The writing standards for Grades 9–10 focus on incorporating more details from source materials, as well as describing various events, organizing information in a way that makes sense to readers, and making use of various parts of writing, including vocabulary and structure, to create meaning. Here are some of the main components of the writing standards in these grade levels:

✔ **Argument:** Students pay more attention to detail, accurately use evidence, and adjust their writing based on readers' familiarity with a topic. They continue to work on organization that results in a sense of flow, ensuring that the manner and order in which they present information makes sense to a reader. Students continue to write *objectively* (in an unbiased way) while presenting information and forming a conclusion that adequately reinforces the rest of their writing.

✔ **Information and explanation:** Students use organization and their manner of presentation to support their explanations. This may include how the writing is formatted and how the student incorporates charts, graphs, and other visual aids. The standards continue to emphasize how well students develop information with specific evidence and explain how the major points they are trying to communicate are related to the evidence and resources they use. In writing conclusions, students use what they know from the body of their writing to make statements about the importance of the topic.

✔ **Narrative:** The focus in Grades 9–10 includes developing a complex account (fiction or nonfiction) that includes multiple figures (characters or actual people) and story lines. One of the most difficult parts of writing at this level is keeping track of all of the components (such as the people and events). As such, students should pay significant attention to making sure that their narrative develops naturally and in a way that is understandable to readers.

Students continue to build their research skills in order to answer questions, including a research question or hypothesis they come up with on their own. They also keep searching for, identifying, and selecting appropriate and trustworthy sources, evaluating those sources to understand which ones are best for their particular area of research. With the increased reliance on research, properly formatting citations is a skill students continue to use in Grades 9–10. The standards indicate that students should apply writing skills in this grade band to the recommendations for literature and texts mentioned in the reading standards for Grades 9–10. (See the section on reading standards for a summary of this content.)

# Grades 11–12

As the final set of writing standards for students in high school, the skills in Grades 11–12 pull together all of the components of writing from previous grade levels into a complex set of expectations. Take a glance at a few of the key aspects of the writing standards:

✔ **Argument:** Students make specific, well-reasoned, and substantially supported arguments. Students' writings also demonstrate the importance of organization for clear communication, acknowledge opposing viewpoints, and take an unbiased look at evidence that supports both sides of an argument.

✔ **Information and explanation:** One of the added components in the standards for this grade band involves organizing information so that a student's writing adds to, strengthens, clarifies, and/or supports previous sections. This includes using appropriate vocabulary and figurative language to support a potential reader's understanding of the topic.

✔ **Narrative:** Students continue to write complex accounts of events while also capturing a reader's attention, presenting the points of view of various characters and/or individuals, and developing the plot (and subplots) throughout the course of their writing. Students add to their abilities to write about events by writing with a specific tone. This may result in writing that evokes feelings such as tension or curiosity, depending on the events in the story.

Students in Grades 11–12 continue to use technology to distribute their writing, using a blog or some other type of website to post writing that can be changed based on remarks from others. The research skills used by students in Grades 9–10 are extended in Grades 11–12, particularly in terms of a student's ability to use material from various credible sources without using too much information from a single source. As with the previous grade band, students are expected to apply the writing skills in Grades 11–12 to the recommended literature and texts from the reading standards.

# Mastering the Spoken Word: Speaking and Listening

Building on the speaking and listening skills developed in kindergarten through Grade 5, the standards in Grades 6–12 continue to support students in their ability to engage with peers in conversations based on specific texts, ideas, and concepts. The expectations of student presentations also expand in these grades as the content and style of presentations grows more complex. In this section, I cover some of the expectations for speaking and listening in each grade level.

# Grade 6

In Grade 6, students take part in conversations that vary in format, including talking with one other student, discussing a topic in groups, and participating in an activity that is facilitated by the teacher. Regardless of the structure, students should study relevant information in advance so they are ready to play an active role in the conversation. When collaborating with partners, students are expected to establish goals and a timeline for completion (if they are working on a project) and understand the responsibilities of the group members. Within conversation, students dive into details and ask one another questions that require specific evidence and explanations. When speaking to others, students should make eye contact and speak at a pace and volume that others can understand. If visual aids, data, or other representations of information are used, students need to be able to make sense of those, as well. Regardless of the type or format of evidence introduced, students should be able to tell whether it supports a specific position. When presenting material, students should make use of key facts and details, along with any visual aids or other mediums.

The Common Core Standards assume that students will follow the conventions of the English language in formal speech and writing. The next section of this chapter has an overview of those standards.

# Grade 7

The speaking and listening standards for Grade 7 include many of the skills introduced in Grade 6, while also introducing a variety of new expectations. Students learn to track their own progress when working toward established goals and to monitor the group to get back on track when discussion wanders off topic. When listening to others speak, students take into consideration the information they hear and consider how it may make them refine their own perspective. They also determine whether someone has accurately interpreted a source used in support of his or her statements. When presenting information, students focus on the most important aspects of their presentation and use some type of visual aid or other mediums to underscore the significance of what they're presenting.

# Grade 8

In Grade 8, students continue to use prior research, and incorporate that information into conversations. When working in groups, students practice making decisions as a group. They also synthesize information presented by multiple people and make adjustments to or defend their position based on the material that is presented. They begin to examine *why* a speaker chooses to use certain information, along with making note of how well evidence is used and whether any of the information is irrelevant. Students continue making presentations that are understandable and well organized and that make effective use of supporting facts and details. They are also asked to incorporate forms of mediums that may make their presentations more interesting.

# Grades 9–10

In Grades 9–10, students use prior research in discussion even more. So it is imperative that students approach conversation and collaboration with partners forearmed with understanding of what they have read. The guidelines for working with other students become more complex, and students are expected to make group decisions that reach as much consensus as possible in an effort to meet established goals. In group discussions, students ask questions that stimulate further conversation, that make connections with the ideas of others, and that clarify what has been said. Another expectation is that students carefully consider information that is presented so they can point out when sources and evidence have been misconstrued. When presenting information, students make sure that others can understand their main points and use various mediums to support important aspects of their presentation.

# Grades 11–12

Students in Grades 11–12 continue to draw on research and evidence when they enter into conversations, making sure that discussions are based on relevant evidence. A point of emphasis at this level is ensuring that students are polite and fair when they are discussing their points of view and allow for everyone to be heard. This is important because hearing from a variety of viewpoints allows for new ways of thinking that may have been previously overlooked. After hearing a presentation, students identify when more information is needed on a particular topic. They also analyze how others use content, style, organization, and sources of information in presentations. When doing their own research, students continue using sources that are appropriate for a given topic, and they are able to point out when sources don't agree. Based on evidence found in sources, students develop a stance that is understandable and that makes sense for the purpose of the presentation. Students continue to use visual aids and other mediums to support their goals for a presentation.

# Exploring Higher-Level Rules and Conventions of Language

In the language standards for Grades 6–12, students receive further guidance on proper usage of grammar and other conventions of the English language. Because the standards are so specific, I provide just a sample of what to expect in each grade. For a full listing of the standards and the skills and concepts included, visit www.corestandards.org.

Don't forget to check out Appendix A of the English language arts standards. You'll find additional information on the skills addressed in each grade.

## Grade 6

In Grade 6, students extend their understanding and use of different types of pronouns, add variety to the structure of sentences used, and extend their familiarity of new and different words. Here's a sampling of some of the skills and concepts from Grade 6:

- ✔ Understand *subjective* (identifies the subject of a sentence), *objective* (identifies the object of a sentence), and *possessive* (shows a relationship or possession) pronouns.

- ✔ Use punctuation, such as commas and dashes, to separate parts of a sentence.

- ✔ Use resources such as dictionaries to determine the proper pronunciation of words.

✔ Anticipate a word's meaning using available clues, and check for accuracy.

✔ Tell the difference between a word's *connotative* meaning (what it is commonly associated with or thought to infer) and its *denotative* meaning (the dictionary definition).

 At the end of each section of language standards, a final standard indicates that students should use vocabulary words and other phrases that are specific to their grade and subjects. Some of these words vary from location to location, so check with your child's teacher for a list of important words and phrases for each class.

## Grade 7

Students in Grade 7 apply previously and newly learned concepts to write more complex sentences. They also continue to use their skills in discerning the meaning of terms as they incorporate new words into their analysis of texts. Take a look at a few of the skills and concepts addressed in Grade 7:

✔ Identify *clauses* and why they are used in sentences.

✔ Avoid *dangling modifiers.*

✔ Use commas with *coordinate adjectives* (adjectives that modify the same noun in similar ways), such as writing that it has been a "long, tiring day."

✔ Understand the meaning of *figures of speech* (a word or phrase with a familiar connotative meaning, such as something that makes reference to a well-known piece of literature).

✔ Tell the difference between words that have similar meanings (denotations) but different connotations.

## Grade 8

The emphasis in Grade 8 includes using various forms of verbs to vary the style and tone of writing. Students also identify when verbs are used incorrectly, such as a shift in verb tense. Here's a brief selection of the skills and concepts addressed in Grade 8:

✔ Understand the use of *verbals*, which are verbs that have been altered to form a new word that functions as a different part of speech, such as the subject or direct object. For example, *gerunds* are verbals that are formed by adding *–ing* to verbs and that function as nouns. For example, in the statement "walking is a healthy activity," the word *walking* is a gerund that serves as the subject of the sentence.

✔ Write using the active and passive voice. *Active voice* involves the subject carrying out the action described by the verb, such as "The dog ate the bone." *Passive voice* occurs when the subject receives the action of the sentence, such as "The bone was eaten by the dog."

✔ Use different moods in writing, including *indicative* (stating a fact), *imperative* (stating a request or demand), *interrogative* (asking a question), *conditional* (indicating that one thing relies on another), and *subjunctive* (indicating a hypothetical situation).

✔ Continue to use context clues, root words, and other cues to understand the meaning of figurative language, affixes, and other unknown or difficult language.

# Grades 9–10

The standards for Grades 9–10 involve adding a variety of structure and tone to writing, along with formalizing processes for citing source material. Students also encounter increasingly complex and detailed approaches to understanding and using specific vocabulary, figures of speech, and other types of language. These are some of the expectations:

✔ Understand and use *parallel structure*. This involves using words in the same form, such as saying "Jim likes to read, write, and talk." A sentence such as "Jim likes to read, write, and talking" is not parallel because the verbs don't match up.

✔ Write using different types of phrases, including adjective phrases (such as *really tall*) and adverbial phrases (such as *very fast*), and clauses, such as dependent and independent clauses. An *independent clause* expresses a complete thought using a subject and verb (for example, "Joe ran to his house"); whereas, a *dependent clause* has a subject and verb but does not express a complete thought (for example, "While Joe ran to his house").

✔ Incorporate colons (:) and semicolons (;).

✔ Use formal citation guides, such as Modern Language Association (MLA), American Psychological Association (APA), and Turabian, in writing and editing.

✔ Examine how figures of speech, such as oxymorons, are used in writing and what they accomplish.

# Grades 11–12

In Grades 11–12, students dive into the details of style and its many nuances. Using what they learned in previous grade levels, students are able to discern the meaning of unknown words using context clues and their prior knowledge about root words, affixes, and figures of speech. Here are a few of the expectations for Grades 11–12:

✔ Recognize that matters of convention are subject to time and place, meaning that the "right" or "accepted" way isn't always the same even though there is presently a standard for writing conventions in the English language.

✔ Use hyphens (-) correctly.

✔ Use different kinds of syntax (how sentences are written in terms of order and structure) in writing as a means of changing styles.

✔ Grasp the meaning of figures of speech, such as hyperbole, in context.

## Tracking language progressive skills

Within the English language arts standards, you'll find the "language progressive skills." These skills are presented in the form of a chart that indicates at which grade various language skills are addressed by the standards. Although these skills are represented in the standards for each grade, the language progressive skills provide a quick and efficient way to identify at which grades certain skills are taught.

# Chapter 9

# Mastering Literacy in History/Social Studies, Science, and Technical Subjects

· · · · · · · · · · · · · · · · · · · · · · · · · · · · · · · · · · · · ·

## In This Chapter

▶ Leaping into literacy in history/social studies

▶ Tackling texts in science and technical subjects

▶ Wrapping up with writing skills

· · · · · · · · · · · · · · · · · · · · · · · · · · · · · · · · · · · · ·

*D*uring the course of his school career, your child will take numerous courses in social studies, science, and other disciplines beyond math and English language arts. The reading and writing he does in these classes highlights some of the most interesting and engaging topics he'll ever encounter. These courses may even influence the career field your child chooses. Your child can devour a feast of exciting information, if he has the proper tools.

This chapter provides an overview of the reading and writing standards for history/social studies, science, and technical subjects, more commonly referred to as the literacy standards. Unlike the standards for math and English language arts, these standards don't define exactly *what* a student should know. Instead, the literacy standards outline expectations for *how* a student should use reading and writing skills to navigate complex texts and develop detailed writing assignments in a variety of subjects.

The literacy standards are used in Grades 6–12 as students move into more specialized courses in these subject areas. You're probably familiar with courses in history/social studies and science, but the phrase *technical subjects* may be new to you. The standards aren't specific about what qualifies as a technical subject, but generally they are courses in career and technical fields, such as automotive mechanics, agriculture, and computer science, that rely on complex procedures and various uses of data.

The literacy standards are divided into two sections of reading standards (one for history/social studies and one for science and technical subjects) and one unified section of writing standards. Instead of being divided by grade, these standards are grouped into three grade bands: Grades 6–8, 9–10, and 11–12.

# Improving Reading Comprehension in History/Social Studies

The reading standards for history/social studies in Grades 6–12 outline expectations for reading the complex texts students encounter in a history/social studies classroom. For the most part, the standards reference the use of primary and secondary sources in various ways. A *primary source* is a written text or object that originates from the specific point in time being studied. A *secondary source* is a summary or analysis of a primary source. For example, the text of President John F. Kennedy's inaugural address is a primary source, while an article that analyzes his political goals for the speech is a secondary source.

Many of the skills represented in these standards are similar to skills introduced in the reading standards for English language arts, except here they are specifically applied to texts used in history/social studies classes. Your child's reading skills should progress within each grade band.

In the following sections, I highlight the key standards so you'll have a better idea of what to expect. To see a full listing of the standards, visit www.corestandards.org.

# Grades 6–8

In Grades 6–8, students dive into reading complex texts, including primary and secondary sources, and analyzing various aspects of texts, such as vocabulary, the organization of information within a text, and the use of pictures and images.

Keep these skills in mind as you get a handle on the standards in this grade band:

- ✔ Use facts, details, and other evidence in summaries and analyses of texts.

- ✔ Identify the main idea(s) or theme(s) of a text.

- ✔ Describe an event or procedure after reading a text (such as how the number of electoral votes for each state is determined).

- ✔ Recognize how an author's point of view is communicated.

- ✔ Tell the difference between a fact and an opinion.

Although this is just a portion of the skills and concepts addressed in Grades 6–8, they are a good place to start. The best way to support your child in mastering these standards is to put them to practice. Pick out some interesting reading materials for history or other social studies subjects (such as geography or government), and let your child practice one skill at a time when reading. You don't want to overwhelm him or take all the fun out of reading interesting materials, so don't try to do too much at one time.

 Students encounter vocabulary words in many of the texts they read. It's important for them to understand what these words mean so they can comprehend and remember as much of what they read as possible. Keep track of important words by making a list or set of flashcards. Also encourage your child to find the meaning of unfamiliar words when he is reading rather than simply skipping over them.

# Grades 9–10

In Grades 9–10, students continue to focus on the details of a text while also paying attention to when it was written and where it came from. They also take a closer look at the author's purpose, perspective, and techniques for communicating meaning.

Here are a few of the expectations for students in these grades:

✔ Summarize the emergence and progression of specific details in a text, whether it's an idea that arises or an event that takes place.

✔ Distinguish between *causation* and *correlation*. In the former, something happens to make another event happen; in the latter, an event's timing is not the direct result of a preceding event.

✔ Understand how the organization of writing contributes to its meaning and a student's ability to grasp the main points.

✔ Use numerical (quantitative) data and written descriptions (qualitative data) as a means of digging deeper into a specific subject.

✔ Determine how well an author is able to back up what he says in a text.

✔ Analyze how a specific subject is presented and/or portrayed in multiple primary and secondary sources.

As students move into higher grades, they encounter more primary sources that are written in unfamiliar and dated language. For example, a book of eighteenth-century presidential letters may include vocabulary and spellings that aren't common today. Slowly and thoughtfully unpacking these texts is a great way to practice the skills contained in the standards.

## Grades 11–12

In Grades 11–12, students are asked to do even more with the texts they read. The emphasis in these grades shifts to evaluating how and why certain inclusions in a text impact the overall meaning of what was written.

Take a look at some of the skills students encounter in this grade band:

✔ Find and explain the connection between details in a text and the bigger picture of what a text means.

✔ Examine potential reasons why something occurs that are supported by specific evidence from the text.

✔ Determine the various points of view of multiple writers on the same subject and consider how well they support their points of view with details.

✔ Use several sources to research a particular question.

✔ Agree or disagree with information presented in a text based on how well an author uses supporting details.

✔ Pull together research from various sources to grasp the significant ideas and events described within. Students should be able to recognize any differences between the sources.

Much of the emphasis in Grades 11–12 is on managing information from multiple sources. This is a pretty difficult task, and students usually need a lot of practice. One way to help your child master these skills is to find three texts that address a similar topic, such as a political speech on a new initiative and two newspaper editorials on the initiative (one supporting and one opposing). After reading the political speech and identifying key details, your child can then read the two editorials and analyze the arguments and opinions presented by all three writers.

# Deciphering Texts on Scientific and Technical Topics

Many of the same skills outlined in the reading standards for history/social studies are also addressed in the reading standards for science and technical subjects. However, the standards reflect the use of scientific content, and in many cases can be used in a laboratory setting or a classroom arrangement that is focused on the completion of a complicated project.

Reading complex texts, citing evidence to back up thoughts regarding the meaning of texts, and making sense of how a text is structured in order to add meaning to what is being said are all significant components of the standards in this section. The following sections identify some of the other major concepts included in these standards.

## Grades 6–8

Many of the reading skills for science and technical subjects are similar to those in history/social studies. One of the major exceptions is that students use these standards with texts that describe and explain complicated scientific and technical processes, so they need to take time to understand what they read.

Here are a few of the skills addressed in Grades 6–8:

✔ Summarize a text objectively.

✔ Carry out a procedure with several steps.

✔ Examine reasons why an author includes certain information, such as details about a specific part of a text.

✔ Use visuals to represent other forms of information, such as numerical data or descriptions.

✔ Recognize whether conclusions are supported by evidence with a text or other forms of research.

✔ Find similarities and differences between information gathered from reading materials and other forms of mediums.

Science classes in Grades 6–8 often cover a range of attention-grabbing topics, including the earth's physical processes, chemical reactions, and many interesting environments and creatures. There's no reason science should be a boring subject for your child. Spend some time talking to your child about scientific topics that interest him and then work together to locate interesting reading material with which to practice his reading skills.

## Grades 9–10

As students move into Grades 9–10, the classes they take in science and technical subjects become more complicated. Along with that, they encounter reading materials that are more and more complex and that require greater attention to precision and detail as they read and carry out procedures.

Take a look at some of the expectations for students in Grades 9–10:

✔ Follow how something is described and developed with details over the course of a text.

✔ Examine how significant concepts are organized in writing and how important words are related.

✔ Along with determining the reasons why an author wrote certain information, identify the main question that was the author's reason for writing.

✔ Write a description of numerical or visual data in words and convert numerical data or written information into a visual display.

✔ Determine similarities and differences between various sources, along with identifying which sources are supported by other texts or experiments.

To reinforce the attention to detail that is needed for reading texts in science and technical subjects in Grades 9–10, let your child practice summarizing the necessary steps in complex procedures. Using some of the reading materials he brings home from school, have him explain the steps in his own words. This can help remove some of the stigma of difficulty associated with lab and project-based procedures.

# Grades 11–12

Students in Grades 11–12 encounter scientific and technical texts that are more complex than any they've previously read. Similarly, the expectations for what they will be able to do after they've read these texts are also more demanding than in earlier grade levels. Make sure your child continues to progress and doesn't get frustrated as he works to discern meaning from various texts.

One way you can check his progress is to determine whether he is struggling with the actual reading of the texts or is simply confused by some of the content. If your child seems to understand the concepts when you talk with him, there's a pretty good chance that he is struggling with the complexity of the text. If this becomes a pattern, take it slow and ask him to read the text aloud while identifying unfamiliar or difficult words. It's important for your child to understand that he can dissect hard-to-read texts if he takes his time, doesn't get stuck on unknown vocabulary, and takes advantage of resources such as a dictionary, thesaurus, or the Internet.

A few of the skills represented in these standards include:

✔ Identify when a text doesn't contain significant information or is lacking in some way.

✔ Advance in demonstrating an understanding of a text by moving from providing summaries to paraphrasing what's been read.

✔ After carrying out a procedure, examine the outcome and compare it to written descriptions of what should have occurred.

✔ See how a text organizes information into a specific category or in order of importance.

✔ Determine places in a text where something is unclear or inconclusive.

✔ Pull together and use various forms of data and information when answering a question or conducting research.

# Reading within the grade bands

The reading standards for history/social studies, science, and technical subjects don't tell students *what* they should read but rather *how* they should use reading skills to fully comprehend a text. Because these standards are grouped into grade bands, you may be confused about how these standards are used. Basically, teachers apply the reading standards to the content and related reading materials for each course. A Grade 7 science teacher may use the reading standards for Grades 6–8 and apply the skills to specific lessons and activities. For example, he may choose an article that describes how pollution affects the process of photosynthesis in a certain plant. Students may be asked to read the article, identifying important information and key details (as outlined by the reading standards for science and technical subjects for Grades 6–8). Then the teacher may have the students organize their information into an argumentative essay in the form of a newspaper editorial, drawing from the writing standards for Grades 6–8, that outlines the harmful effects of pollution on local plant life and on the community.

It's important to understand the role of Standard 10 in each set of reading standards. Standard 10 ensures that students are reading texts that are appropriately complex for each grade level. Although the content of reading materials may vary, the standards outline expectations for complexity (whether quantitative or qualitative) that serve as guidelines for each grade. See the sidebar on text complexity in Chapter 7 or Appendix A of the English language arts standards for more information.

# Writing about History/Social Studies, Science, and Technical Subjects

One unified set of writing standards applies to history/social studies, science, and technical subjects. The structure and content of these standards closely resemble the writing standards for English language arts, including an emphasis on three purposes for writing: argue, inform/explain, and narrate. However, unlike the writing standards for English language arts, the literacy standards for these subjects don't contain a separate strand for narrative writing. The expectation is that narrative writing is addressed in students' argumentative and informative or explanatory writing because they describe how an event unfolds or a specific process or procedure works. If you think about it, this makes sense for these subjects.

Another difference between the two sets of writing standards is that the topics students write about in history/social studies, science, and technical subjects are specific to the subject being studied. So, as your child moves from grade to grade, the writing he does in these classes increases in complexity and changes to fit the content he is studying in each class.

The writing standards for these subjects are grouped into the following grade bands:

- ✔ Grades 6–8
- ✔ Grades 9–10
- ✔ Grades 11–12

Note that the writing standards for English language arts are separate for Grades 6, 7, and 8 but are combined into a Grade 6–8 band in the literacy standards. You'll notice that the writing standards for this grade band most closely resemble the writing standards for Grade 8 in the English language arts standards. That's because the expectations of the grade band are reflective of where students should be when they reach the end of Grade 8.

Don't forget that students' abilities will vary. Because the standards cover more than one grade level, you need to keep a close eye on your child's progress to ensure that he is mastering new skills. If your child is in a grade level on the lower end of a grade band, reach out to your child's teacher if you want a more specific list of skills that he can practice for his grade level.

# Part III

# Part of Tens

Read ten things you need to know about assessments at www.
dummies.com/extras/commoncoreforparents.

## In this part. . .

✔ Take a look at important questions to ask your child's teacher.

✔ Review key strategies to help your child master the Common Core Standards.

# Chapter 10

# Ten Tips for Parents

As a parent, you're likely to wonder what your child is doing in school and whether she's acquiring the knowledge and skills she needs to succeed in the next grade and ultimately in life after high school. You don't want to be a helicopter parent hovering over your child in class, but you do have a responsibility to know your child's academic strengths and weaknesses, whether she's meeting academic expectations in school, and what you can do at home to play a supportive role.

Of course, you can and should ask your child what she's working on, how well she's doing in her classes, and whether she needs help in any subjects, but you may not get straight answers or the details you need to take any necessary action. You need to supplement the responses you get from your child with objective observations and insight from your child's teacher(s). This chapter lists ten essential questions to ask in order to elicit the information and insight you need, along with explanations of why you should ask these questions and what you should do in response to the answers you receive.

# What's My Child Currently Working On?

One of the best opening questions you can ask your child's teacher is, "What's my child currently working on?" Knowing the concepts and skills that are the focus of study enable you to

- Identify the standards that apply to this area of study
- Ask your child more focused questions about what she's doing at school
- Start to develop ideas on what you can do at home to support your child

# How Well Is My Child Meeting Expectations?

A teacher's overall sense of how well your child is mastering the concepts and skills required in a certain subject area is likely to provide greater insight into how your child is doing than you can glean from progress and grade reports. For example, some students who've mastered a certain topic may not hand in their homework assignments. Other students may raise their grade by doing extra-credit assignments but may not really grasp the subject.

 If a child's grades don't match up with her knowledge and skills in a particular subject area, find out why so you know which problem to address. If your child just doesn't get it, that's an entirely different problem than if she's not turning in her homework.

# May I See Samples of My Child's Work?

Progress reports and grades may not be a clear indication of the quality of your child's work. To see what your child is turning in and gauge the quality of her work, ask her teacher the following questions:

> ✔ May I see samples of my child's work?
>
> ✔ What do you think about the quality of these samples?
>
> ✔ What criteria do you use to measure the quality of work?

By looking at samples of your child's work, you can often determine whether she's performing up to her potential. The answers to these questions also enable you to gauge classroom expectations and understand the criteria for quality at this grade level.

# Is My Child Struggling in Any Subject Areas?

You can't address an issue you don't know about, so ask your child's teachers to let you know as early as possible whether your child is struggling with any concept or skill. The earlier you can get your child the help she needs in clarifying a concept or developing a skill, the better the outcome.

Many schools have technology that enables parents to check their children's progress online. You may be able to check progress reports, grades, missed assignments, disciplinary actions, and so forth. Remain vigilant, especially if your child lacks self-motivation.

If your child repeatedly struggles and you have reason to suspect that she may have a learning disability, ask whether your school system has screening processes to identify any problems. Children who have learning disabilities or other factors that inhibit their ability to learn are often eligible for classroom accommodations that can curb the negative effects of these disabilities. Reach out to your child's teachers for more information.

The Common Core Standards are designed to encourage progression in a stair-step fashion. Knowledge and skills acquired in one grade build upon knowledge and skills mastered in the previous grade. Falling behind requires extra effort to catch up.

# In Which Subject Areas Does My Child Excel?

Some students are incredibly gifted and driven to excel in certain academic areas, such as English, math, or science. You need to know which subject areas these are as much as you need to know the areas in which your child struggles, so you can

✔ Encourage and support your child in pursing her interests and developing her special abilities

✔ Help your child plan a path for future success that makes the most of her abilities

✔ Harness her success in one area of study to encourage success in other areas of pursuit

# What Can I Do to Help My Child Achieve the Standards?

Although I present guidance and activities you can use to support your child at home in achieving the Common Core Standards, your child's teacher is likely to have a host of her own ideas and suggestions. Most teachers are more than happy to tap the power of involved parents in stimulating a student's interest and providing the student with the support and resources she needs to excel. After all, student success reflects positively on the teacher's performance.

# If My Child Needs Help with Homework, What Resources Are Available?

Parents aren't always the most qualified to help a student master a certain concept or develop a skill. Even if at some point in time you knew how to solve polynomial equations and calculate the heat given off by a certain chemical reaction, you've likely forgotten. That's perfectly understandable.

If you can't recall what you've learned, you don't feel confident explaining a particular concept, or you don't have the patience to deal with your own kid, ask the teacher for other resources and forms of assistance, including the following:

- ✔ Online tutorials
- ✔ Online homework helper sites
- ✔ Tutors (teachers or students)
- ✔ Homework helplines

Encourage your child to bookmark the best resources for return visits, and don't forget YouTube, which has video lectures and demonstrations in all subject areas in which your child is likely to need help.

# Does the School Offer Any Opportunities for Academic Enrichment?

Most schools offer learning opportunities outside the classroom, such as the following:

- ✔ School newspaper
- ✔ Yearbook committee
- ✔ Clubs, such as the chess club, science club, math club, and foreign language club
- ✔ Book clubs
- ✔ Academic Decathlon
- ✔ Band and choir
- ✔ Theater

All of these activities (and more) stimulate brain cells and help students develop social and communication skills. Athletic activities help in these areas, as well, but they get enough press already. Even if your child is very involved in athletics, encourage her to look into other, more-academic extracurricular activities.

# What Can My Child Be Doing to Develop Good Study Habits?

Although Common Core Standards establish the overarching goals of K–12 education, good study habits to achieve those goals and succeed after graduation are still essential. Good study habits empower students to become lifelong learners as they become familiar with the approach to learning new concepts and skills.

Ask your child's teacher whether he or she has any suggestions for what your child needs to do to develop good study habits. Perhaps the school or your school district's parent-teacher association (PTA) offers a workshop for parents and students. Maybe the school has an orientation program that includes a section on study habits, or maybe your child's teacher can recommend an online resource.

As essential as good study habits are to student success, many school systems have no courses on how to establish good study habits. Expect the worst, be prepared to explore resources outside of your child's school, and be pleasantly surprised and grateful if your school district explicitly teaches effective study habits.

# Which Classes Should My Child Be Taking

By the beginning of high school, you and your child should start thinking about your child's academic abilities, interests, and goals and planning how to get from point A to point B, whether that point B is a college, trade school, or specific career path.

Team up with teachers, school counselors, and your child to find out where your child's interests and abilities are leading and draw up a plan for which courses your child needs to take to prepare her for the next step in her journey to success upon graduation from high school. Careful preparation ensures a smooth transition from high school to college or career.

# Chapter 11

# Ten Ways to Help Your Child Achieve Common Core Standards

•••••••••••••••••••••••••••••••••••••••••••••••

## In This Chapter

▶ Staying on top of assignments

▶ Sustaining a productive home environment

▶ Finding a proper balance of support

▶ Rewarding effort during challenges and successes

▶ Taking advantage of opportunities for growth

•••••••••••••••••••••••••••••••••••••••••••••••

*M*ost parents want to send their children to school confident that they are acquiring the knowledge and skills they need to succeed in college and career. That expectation is certainly reasonable. After all, doctors are expected to relieve ailments; mechanics, to fix cars; and pilots, to fly planes. Surely, teachers should educate children.

But education is different. It works best when approached as a collaborative effort between home and school that involves the joint efforts of school administrators, teachers, parents, and, of course, students. As a parent, you play a key role in your child's academic achievement. Your job is to make sure that your child receives a quality education, exerts the effort required to reach her academic potential, obtains the guidance she needs to set a path for success, and has the educational resources required to stimulate her brain.

This chapter provides ten concrete ways that you, as a parent, can help your child achieve the Common Core Standards.

# Know What Your Child Is Working on

As a parent, be aware of what your child is studying at school. To support your child's understanding of essential skills and concepts, you need to be up to speed on what is happening in the classroom. Here are a few ideas that will help you stay current on the topics she is studying:

- ✔ Check to see whether your child's teacher has a website or newsletter that communicates important upcoming assignments.

- ✔ Take a look at the major topics addressed in homework and/or graded assignments that are sent home.

- ✔ Regularly carry on conversations with your child about specific skills and concepts she studies at school.

- ✔ Review the Common Core Standards for relevant grade levels/subjects so that you have an idea of what your child will be learning all year.

- ✔ Ask your child's teacher for a list of upcoming topics so you can familiarize yourself with important content.

Taking the time to try out a few of these ideas helps you stay in touch with specific material that your child is learning. You need to be in the know so you can help her out with challenging content.

# Monitor Your Child's Performance

As an involved parent, you want to keep tabs on how well your child is progressing at school. If you don't receive frequent and consistent communication from your child's teacher, this can be frustrating. However, you can take action to make this process easier. Asking yourself the following questions helps you think through your plan for successfully monitoring your child's performance at school:

✔ Does my child receive graded assignments that I can review on a specific day of the week?

✔ Is there an online grade portal where I can see all of my child's grades at once?

✔ How can I determine my child's cumulative grade/ average in a particular class?

 Some teachers and schools use traditional numerical averages and letter grades, while others use a method known as standards-based grading. Standards-based grading involves tracking student mastery on specific skills and concepts so that more emphasis is placed on what a student knows rather than the number or letter grade attached to it.

✔ Is there a way I can monitor how well my child understands certain skills and concepts before a test is given?

✔ What can I do after receiving results from a test to help her in any areas where she may have struggled?

# Have a Daily Homework/ Study Routine

It's important to model consistency for your child, especially when it comes to responsibilities like schoolwork. Have conversations about the importance of getting into routines and developing good habits, especially for completing homework and studying. Work together to develop a schedule that works best for your household. Follow these tips to get started:

✔ Decide whether homework will be done as soon as she gets home or later in the evening.

✔ Think through your weekly schedule and plan ahead for important events.

✔ Make sure an adult is at home to assist with homework if needed.

✔ Leave time for breaks and recreation.

✔ Use this time productively (to read, organize documents, prepare for work, and so on) so your child can see you model attributes such as focus, dedication, and attention to detail.

Although unplanned events pop up every now and then, it's important to stick to the agreed-upon schedule whenever possible.

# Provide a Study-Friendly Environment

It's hard to be efficient and accomplish goals when the environment around you detracts from your productivity and focus. Take this into consideration when you're making decisions about the time, place, and surrounding environment in which your child will study and complete assignments. Use these factors as a checklist for preparing and maintaining an effective environment for schoolwork:

- ✔ Establish a comfortable and inviting environment in which homework can be done.

- ✔ Eliminate distractions, such as loud noises from a TV or radio, from outside, or from other people.

- ✔ Make sure your child has pens, pencils, paper, markers, calculators, and any other necessary resources close at hand.

- ✔ Be on standby to assist your child with challenging problems.

- ✔ Remind your child to organize her workspace before and after she gets started so she can easily access needed materials.

# Don't Do Your Child's Homework!

Although you want your child to complete homework and projects successfully, you need to monitor how much assistance you're giving her. If you provide too much help, you can unintentionally instill a feeling of "learned helplessness."

If that occurs, she'll stop short of sticking with difficult problems because she knows you'll jump in to do the work for her. Here are a few tips to follow:

- ✔ Be available to assist without always feeling the need to jump in as soon as she starts to struggle.

- ✔ Review what she's learning beforehand so you know how to assist when needed.

- ✔ Learn to help her by asking the right questions to prompt her thinking, not by immediately giving her the answer.

It's important to be purposeful about the type of assistance you give to your child on her homework. You want her to see you as a resource who can help clarify her thinking and/or approach but not as someone who is immediately going to give her the answer.

# Praise Your Child's Efforts

Recognizing your child's achievements is important, whether she typically does well in school or has often struggled. If your child generally does well in school, it's easy to think that she will always succeed, and you may forget to praise her accomplishments. On the other hand, if your child struggles in school, sometimes all she hears is negative feedback about how she did something wrong, didn't follow the right steps, and so on. Finding quick and easy ways to provide positive feedback for a job well done is critical, regardless of her typical academic performance. Keep these considerations in mind as you think of ways to reward your child's progress:

- ✔ Focus on rewarding effort and not always basing performance on the numerical or letter grade attached to an assignment.

- ✔ Look at graded assignments in smaller chunks to see whether your child completes certain parts more accurately than others.

- ✔ Find a tangible item, such as edible treats your child likes, that can serve as a quick and easy reward.

✔ Consider allotting additional time on electronic devices such as TVs, computers, tablets, and so on for excellent work at school.

✔ Capitalize on your child's strengths in certain subjects by finding ways to let her further explore topics of interest in which she also displays a high level of aptitude.

# Provide Interesting Reading Material

When you make educational resources available to your child, you transform your home environment into a place that also functions as a learning environment. Keep in mind that students are more likely to stick with a task, such as reading, if they find the material to be interesting and engaging. To make sure this happens, let your child take the lead when looking for reading materials and other resources to be used during her free time. If you have access to the Internet in your home, this is a pretty simple task. Try these tips:

✔ Identify topics of interest to your child and bookmark related web pages on the Internet.

✔ Search for free books that you can download and make readily accessible to your child to read during free time or while you're traveling.

✔ Make use of an Internet-based storage site, such as Dropbox or Google Drive, where reading materials and other resources can be stored and accessed from multiple devices.

If you don't have quick access to the Internet in your home, you can still find a number of ways to put interesting materials in her hands.

✔ Keep your eyes open for free resources in your community that are of interest to your child, such as magazines or leaflets in libraries, museums, and cultural centers, and create a space to store them in your home.

✔ Cut out interesting articles from the newspaper or other printed mediums and store them in a folder that your child can easily access.

✔ Subscribe to a magazine that your child finds interesting.

✔ Check out books from the library and designate a household reading time during which everyone in your family sits down to read something that is interesting.

# Encourage Your Child to Take Advantage of Academic Enrichment Opportunities

Learning occurs in many places outside the four walls of a classroom. Although your child has many school-related responsibilities and obligations, she needs to explore interesting opportunities for academic enrichment. To get started, take a look at the following tips:

✔ Make a list of the academic subjects, career fields, and topics in which your child is interested.

✔ Look at the programs, clubs, and other enrichment opportunities offered by her school.

✔ Research opportunities for involvement with community organizations.

✔ Talk to your child about an appropriate amount of time to allot to these activities, making sure she has enough time for schoolwork.

# Take Fun, Educational Trips

Show your child that educational activities can be fun, interesting, and exciting by taking trips to local libraries, zoos, museums, and other facilities that focus on your child's areas of interest. Keeping education interesting helps your child maintain a spark that drives her to continually explore the world around her. Try this:

✔ Visit your local library on a regular basis, especially when it has special exhibits or programs of interest.

✔ Go to the zoo and participate in a guided tour. Do some research ahead of time and find ways to connect what you'll see at the zoo to your child's classes at school.

✔ Take advantage of museums and the many resources they provide. Look at the museum schedule and pinpoint specific exhibits, tours, and other events that are relevant to what your child is learning at school.

✔ Look into learning experiences that you can take advantage of during vacations. You'll find many interesting locations in popular vacation destinations that can provide memorable learning experiences.

# Encourage Stimulating Hobbies

Although the hobbies your child chooses will depend on her particular interests and talents, keep these questions in mind as you assist her in finding stimulating activities:

✔ Is my child being required to read or write?

✔ Is my child building critical-thinking and problem-solving skills by considering the outcome of multiple scenarios?

✔ Does this hobby require planning and organization?

✔ Is the activity challenging, or just something she can do to pass the time?

✔ Is there a way to connect this hobby to important skills and concepts being addressed at school?

# Appendix

# Resources for the Common Core Standards

● ● ● ● ● ● ● ● ● ● ● ● ● ● ● ● ● ● ● ● ● ● ● ● ● ● ● ● ● ● ● ● ● ● ● ● ● ● ● ● ● ● ● ● ●

*A*s you prepare to help your child tackle the expectations of the Common Core Standards, it's helpful to pull together as many resources as possible. Because of the number of states using the standards, you can look in many places for guidance on the best ways to support your child's education.

In this appendix, I review a few of the national organizations that provide resources related to the Common Core Standards. Although many good resources can be mentioned, I stick to a sampling that gives you a good idea of what is out there. Secondly, I list the states (along with the District of Columbia) that have adopted the Common Core Standards. Many states are vacillating on when and how to implement the standards, so this list represents the information available at the time of publication.

## National Organizations and Parental Resources

Many organizations offer resources related to the Common Core Standards. Here are a few:

> ✔ **Achieve the Core (www.achievethecore.org):** This website, hosted by Student Achievement Partners, contains a significant number of resources for teachers, administrators, policymakers, and parents. Because three of the lead writers of the standards, David Coleman, Jason Zimba, and Susan Pimentel, founded Student Achievement Partners, this site is worth a look.

✔ **Council of Chief State School Officers (www.ccsso.org):** The CCSSO is composed of the leaders of state departments of education. Along with the National Governors Association Center for Best Practices, the CCSSO was one of the organizations that helped lead the effort to create the Common Core Standards. Resources on this site include videos about the standards and other materials related to their implementation.

✔ **Council of the Great City Schools (www.cgcs.org):** Don't let the name fool you. Although the Council of the Great City Schools focuses on supporting education in urban settings, it offers videos and road maps that help unpack the standards for students, teachers, and parents in all locations.

✔ **National Governors Association Center for Best Practices (www.nga.org/cms/center):** Several reports available on the education division of this site are related to the implementation of the Common Core Standards. In cooperation with the CCSSO, this organization worked to coordinate efforts that led to the development of the standards.

✔ **National PTA (www.pta.org):** Your child's school may have an organization that is associated with National PTA. Its website provides numerous resources for parents, including specific grade-by-grade "Guides to Student Success" that are based on the Common Core Standards. The guides identify specific aspects of the standards that you can reinforce at home and provide tips on communicating with your child's teacher.

✔ **Partnership for Assessment of Readiness for College and Careers (www.parcconline.org):** PARCC is one of the two largest assessment consortiums of states working to create assessments for the Common Core Standards. See if your state is a member and view sample assessment items, along with other information related to test administration.

✔ **PBS LearningMedia (www.pbslearningmedia.org):** This site offers a number of resources from various states. From general overviews of the standards to grade- and content-specific material, you'll find a number of good resources that help build your knowledge of the standards.

✔ **Smarter Balanced Assessment Consortium** (www.smart erbalanced.org): Smarter Balanced is one of the two largest consortiums of states that are working together to develop assessments aligned to the Common Core Standards. Visit its website to see if your state is a member and to view other resources, such as sample test items.

# State Departments of Education

At the time of this book's publication, the Common Core State Standards Initiative identifies 45 states and the District of Columbia among the entities that have adopted the standards:

✔ Alabama

✔ Arizona

✔ Arkansas

✔ California

✔ Colorado

✔ Connecticut

✔ Delaware

✔ District of Columbia

✔ Florida

✔ Georgia

✔ Hawaii

✔ Idaho

✔ Illinois

✔ Indiana

✔ Iowa

✔ Kansas

✔ Kentucky

✔ Louisiana

✔ Maine

✔ Maryland

✔ Massachusetts

- ✔ Michigan
- ✔ Mississippi
- ✔ Missouri
- ✔ Montana
- ✔ Nevada
- ✔ New Hampshire
- ✔ New Jersey
- ✔ New Mexico
- ✔ New York
- ✔ North Carolina
- ✔ North Dakota
- ✔ Ohio
- ✔ Oklahoma
- ✔ Oregon
- ✔ Pennsylvania
- ✔ Rhode Island
- ✔ South Carolina
- ✔ South Dakota
- ✔ Tennessee
- ✔ Utah
- ✔ Vermont
- ✔ Washington
- ✔ West Virginia
- ✔ Wisconsin
- ✔ Wyoming

# Index

## • Y •

## • Z •

# About the Author

**Dr. Jared Myracle** is an instructional supervisor in the Gibson County Special School District in Tennessee and an adjunct instructor at Union University in Jackson, Tennessee. He also has experience as a classroom teacher and a school administrator. He works alongside other educators in Tennessee to guide the implementation of the Common Core Standards as a member of the Tennessee Department of Education's Common Core Leadership Council. He is also a member of the Expect More Achieve More Advisory Council and a board member for the Tennessee Rural Education Association.

# Dedication

This book is dedicated to the tireless efforts of my parents, Andy and Beth, and grandparents, Margaret and Clenon, Wanda and Chuck, to support the education of their children, grandchildren, and great-grandchildren. I could ask for no better examples of sacrifice and selflessness in the interest of their families.

# Author's Acknowledgments

This book is the outcome of contributions from many individuals. Special thanks to Lindsay Lefevere, executive editor, and Joe Kraynak, who helped me conceptualize the scope of this project and take my first steps as an author. Thanks are also in order to Tracy Brown, my project editor, and Ashley Petry, my copy editor, who patiently worked with me as chapters took shape and neared completion.

Acknowledgments for this book would not be complete without mentioning several colleagues whose efforts to increase student achievement drove conversations around the implementation and use of the Common Core Standards long before this book was written. My friend and co-worker Rory Hinson and my colleagues on Tennessee's Common Core Leadership Council are all first-rate educators whose insight, perspective, and passion are truly changing lives.

## Publisher's Acknowledgments

**Executive Editor:** Lindsay Lefevere

**Assistant Editor:** David Lutton

**Project Editor:** Tracy Brown Hamilton

**Copy Editor:** Ashley Petry

**Technical Editor:** Leslie Arceneaux

**Art Coordinator:** Alicia B. South

**Project Coordinator:** Phillip Midkiff

**Cover Photos:** ©iStockphoto.com/ma_rish